AMERICAN RACE RELATIONS TODAY

AMERICAN RACE
RELATIONS TODAY

EDITED BY EARL RAAB

ANCHOR BOOKS
Doubleday & Company, Inc.
Garden City, New York

The Anchor Books edition is the first publication of *American Race Relations Today*.

Anchor Books edition: 1962

Library of Congress Catalog Card Number 62–15926

ACKNOWLEDGMENTS

The abridgements of "The Sit-Ins and the New Negro Students" by Charles U. Smith (The Journal of Intergroup Relations, Summer, 1961); "Mexicans in the United States" by Leonard Broom and Eshref Shevky (Journal of Sociology and Social Research, January-February, 1952); "The Adjustment of Puerto Ricans to New York City" by Joseph P. Fitzpatrick (Journal of Intergroup Relations, Winter 1959–60) are printed here with the permission of the publishers and the approval of the authors. The edited selections from *Slums and Suburbs: A Commentary on Schools in Metropolitan Areas,* by James B. Conant (McGraw-Hill Book Company, Inc., Copyright © 1961 by James Bryant Conant) which appears here under the title, "Schools and Negro Slums" is reprinted here by permission of the author, publisher and the Educational Testing Service which administers the studies being conducted by Dr. Conant. The edited selections from *The Black Muslims in America* by C. Eric Lincoln (Beacon Press, Copyright © 1961 by C. Eric Lincoln); and from *Prejudice and Society* by Earl Raab and Seymour Martin Lipset (Anti-Defamation League of Bnai Brith, 1959), which appears here under the title, "The Prejudiced Society," are printed here by permission of the authors and publishers. "Changing Social Roles in the New South" by Joseph Himes (Southwestern Social Science Quarterly); "The Metropolitan Area as a Social Problem" by Morton Grodzins (University of Pittsburgh Press, 1958); "Can Intergroup Quotas Be Benign"

5

Acknowledgments

by Dan Dodson (Journal of Intergroup Relations, Autumn, 1960); and "Is 'Integration' Possible in New York Schools" by Nathan Glazer (Commentary, 1960, Copyright American Jewish Committee) are reprinted here with permission of the publishers and the authors.

Contents

7

Contents

AMERICAN RACE RELATIONS TODAY

Introduction

Progress can be described as the movement from simpler problems to more complex problems. The recent development of race relations in the United States has been just such a record of progress. As a result, the relatively straightforward remedies of the current civil rights revolution are no longer considered adequate.

In the fifteen-year period following World War II, twenty-one states passed enforceable laws prohibiting discrimination in public and private employment. About 98 per cent of the non-white population outside the South is now covered by such a law. The rest of the civil rights legislative agenda seems to follow in train behind this basic "fair employment" statute. In the same period, sixteen states enacted a prohibition of one kind or another against discrimination in housing. At each state legislative session these housing laws are generally broadened, as are the sanctions against discrimination in public accommodations, on the books of the twenty-seven states. At least eight states created over-all commissions against discrimination to enforce these networks of law, thus establishing themselves as active partisans against inequality based on racial, religious or ethnic identity.

The civil rights revolution necessarily addressed itself in other terms to the interracial problems of the Southern states where upward movement began from a different historical floor. Seven of these states passed "anti-lynch," "anti-masking," or other laws to hobble the uninhibited operations of the Ku-Klux Klan. Congress adopted its first civil rights bill in eighty-two years, establishing federal civil rights agencies and specifically enabling the federal government to enjoin violations of voting rights anywhere in the country. The Supreme Court invalidated racially restricted juries, restrictive real estate covenants, "white primaries," segregated public schools and segregated public transportation. The executive branch of the federal government desegregated the armed services and ruled out business with any contractor whose employment policy was discriminatory.

This was a governmental revolution, executed by official society either through new legislation or through judicial or administrative reinterpretation of existing law. For the Southern situation, it was still largely a matter of removing the historical debris of discriminatory law. For the rest of the country, it was the building of a brand-new structure of anti-discriminatory law. But both movements shared the same drummer and together comprised a dazzling legal revolution. The seeds of this revolution were sown at the turn of the century, in the rise of the industrial North; and in the social and economic decline of the post-Reconstruction South.

The subordination of the Negroes had never run a steady course. In Colonial America, the position of the Negro slave was not too different from that of the indentured white servant. The institution of slavery was weakening perceptibly until the cotton market opened up and the cotton gin made its appearance. It was at this point, at the beginning of the nineteenth century, that modern American racism was born as a rationalization for maintaining Negro slavery. The ideology of "Negro inferiority" was developed. The subordinate status of the Negro was systematized for the first time. This system of oppression was briefly wiped out after the Civil War, but economic and political interests swept it back with new force. At the end of the nineteenth century were enacted racially oppressive laws unprecedented in the South, legally imposing segregation and second-class citizenship at every level of public life.

Negroes moved to the labor-hungry North with the standard disadvantages of any large migrant group which was relatively underskilled, undereducated, and culturally alien. All such groups suffered periods of social and economic discrimination as they entered into competition with the older layers of society, but in the ferment of American opportunity moved "up" rather quickly. The Negro movement was critically hampered by complications of race and racism, but there was movement.

Over 2 million Negroes left the South for the big cities of the North between 1900 and 1930. The Negro population in New York rose from about 100 thousand to about 350 thousand; in Detroit from 5 thousand to 125 thousand. Between 1940 and 1950 the Negro population in New York City leaped by 300 thousand, in Detroit by 150 thousand. By 1960, there were over a million Negroes in New York City, almost half a million in Detroit. The pattern in every northern and western industrial city was similar. The immigration was, first of all, politically potent. At the turn of the century, Negroes comprised 3 per cent of the New York City population: in 1960, 14 per cent. In 1900, less than 2 per cent of the Detroit population were Negroes; in 1960, over 28 per cent. Formidable pools of voting strength had gathered in the metropolitan centers.

But the Negro population was not just moving into the North, and into the cities; it was also edging into the mainstream of the American industrial economy, in response to the urgent needs of that economy. At the beginning of World War II only about 3 per cent of those in war-connected industries were Negro; at the end of the war about 8 per cent in these industries were Negro, approaching the percentage of Negroes in the general population. The proportion of non-white males employed as skilled craftsmen more than doubled between 1940 and 1960, while the proportion of white males working as skilled craftsmen increased by only a quarter. The proportion of white males in clerical and sales jobs remained the same during that period while the proportion of non-white males more than tripled. The income of the Negro worker rose by more than fourfold while the white worker's income was increasing threefold. The Negro was a man in motion. And there was a global war with all its root-shaking dislocations—a war fought ideologically against racism, in which Negroes participated, under the impact of which a Negro generation grew up, and at the end of which the African revolution began.

New economic and educational mobility, new drives for assertion, new political leverage, and a new world situation for America were elements that fed each other, and burst into the civil rights revolution of the '40s and '50s.

The legal and legislative campaigns of those years also amounted to one of the most deliberate ventures in social engineering ever undertaken by any society. The slogans of the revolution were: Eliminate Discrimination! Eliminate Inequality of Opportunity! Eliminate Segregation! The slogans were and continue to be pertinent to the disadvantaged position of American Negroes and other "minority" groups, but they are also beginning to undershoot the mark.

The Nature of the Problem

Racial subjugation is both a problem in political morality, and a problem in the effective functioning of society. John Dewey commented: "Anything that obscures the

14

fundamentally moral nature of the social problem is harmful."

But while the two aspects of the "race relations question" may not be finally separable, they nevertheless pose somewhat different problems:

1) *As a political and moral problem.* The premise of the American political system is that each man is a sacred individual born afresh with certain inviolable rights by sheer reason of his birth. Among these is his right to be treated as a unique human being; to reap his own rewards and punishments; to fulfill his individual potential without artificial restraint; and, as the founding fathers so drily put it, to follow in the "pursuit of happiness." To deny a man these rights on grounds that are irrelevant to his individual nature and conduct, is immoral and inimical to the political idea which is built around the sanctity of the individual. It has therefore become a burden of government to enjoin that behavior which, through discrimination or segregation, would deny any man equality of opportunity.

2) *As a social problem.* The American society embraces a variety of major groups; sizeable numbers of individuals whose concerted identity may be racial, religious, ethnic or of some other dimension. Their group identity is operational as long as there are major goals and aspirations that are commonly identifiable. These "group aspirations" are often likely to be in conflict, one with another. One test of a society is whether it can tolerate these conflicts, at best grow through them, but at least deal with them rather than be disintegrated by them.

The race-relations problem is partly a conflict in group goals. The aspirations of the Negro community for first-class status are clear. As they have sharpened, so has the interracial conflict. The aspirations held within the white community which would obstruct first-class status for Negroes are not so clear; they tend to be more often indirectly motivated, and more fragmented by region, class and individual bent. But the total weight of these "white" aspirations is sufficient to present a genuine problem in intergroup conflict, most marked in the South, but felt as a national phenomenon. The American society is faced not just with the necessity of actualizing those Negro aspirations to which it is officially committed; but of substantially reconciling the contrary and frustrated aspirations of the white community. At the least, if the social order is to be healthy, the accommodation to Negro aspirations must be accomplished without indefinite recourse to police power, without violence or the constant threat of violence.

In addition, there is the old-chestnut question lingering from those nostalgic days when the nation was preoccupied with "immigrant adjustment": How much integration is necessary for the health and stability of the American society? How much group separatism can the social order tolerate, and still remain an effective social order?

Professor Henry Pratt Fairchild expressed his concern about this problem after World War II,* along with a prophetic reference to the unprecedented global pressures that were about to be exerted on the United States: "The problems of international participation are going to be sufficiently acute and insistent to test all the stability and vitality that the American nation can possess at best, without having it weakened and undermined by dissensions, conflict and disharmonies among more or less irreconcilable elements within its body politic."

Fairchild's specific fears about mass immigration may have been overblown, but he fairly described nationality as "a group of people who feel alike and together about a considerable number of major interests and values of life. They have the same or similar ideas, ideals, aspirations

* Henry Pratt Fairchild, *Race and Nationality*, (New York: Ronald Press, 1947)

and life objectives. They recognize a spiritual, emotional
and intellectual kinship." Cohesion is certainly one of the
defining characteristics of a national society, and in a democratic society at least, this cohesion is presumably built
on shared values and loyalties. But the kinship of shared
values and loyalties is to some extent a product of shared
activities. Cohesion among heterogeneous groups depends
to some extent on their equal participation in community
life. For this purpose, equal opportunity for participation
is not the same as equal participation. For a racial group
to have the open opportunity to attend the same schools,
live in the same neighborhoods, spread across the same
range of economic life as the rest of the community, does
not yet mean that the group in fact attends the same
schools, lives in the same neighborhoods, occupies the
same economic positions in any significant ratio.

A useful if somewhat arbitrary distinction can then be
made between the terms "desegregation" and "integration."
Desegregation removes the bars to integration, provides
equal opportunity to participate. Integration describes the
achievement of a substantial amount of equal group participation. In a broader sense, this is the distinction between equality of opportunity and equality of achievement on a group level.

Desegregation and equality of opportunity protect the
worth and sanctity of the individual and satisfy the imperatives of political morality. They permit any person
who is otherwise qualified to participate and achieve his
personal goals without racial, religious or ethnic disability.
But this does not yet serve all the needs of society. The
fuller development of a sense of community and of cohesion, the fuller utilization of human resources, are directly related to a substantially *realized* integration and
level of achievement for the group.

The civil rights revolution has been primarily concerned

with desegregation and equality of opportunity for the individual on the premise that these will inevitably lead to equal achievement for the group and integration. The past history of ethnic groups in American society would support such a premise. But there is reason for the first time to question the operability of this formula. Despite the civil rights revolution and the decline of racial discrimination on many levels, racial ghettoization is *increasing* in certain unique and significant ways in America.

Well over 3 million Negroes, or about 20 per cent of the total Negro population, live compactly in five large cities of the North and West. They also comprise about 20 per cent of the general population of those cities. These compact centers of Negro population continue to build up in the metropolitan centers, while the white population continues to shift outward. In Detroit, for example, the overall population dropped by about 10 per cent between 1950 and 1960, while the suburbs grew by almost 80 per cent. In New York, the over-all population dropped by about 1 per cent, while the suburbs grew by about 75 per cent. There was a continuing migration of non-whites into the central cities, and a continuing mass exodus of white people from the central cities.

It is no longer possible to say comfortably: Complete the civil rights revolution, end discrimination, and the interracial problem will eventually disappear in the open marketplace of opportunity. Stubbornly separate "black belts" may be deeply rooting themselves in our society, with far-reaching political and social consequences.

The Negro population is characterized by certain statistical group differences which, however extrinsic, are real. The median income of the non-white worker is still little more than half of that of the white worker; seniority and skills are lagging as well as income. There tends to be a statistical difference not only in years of schooling but in educational performance. A survey of school performance of Negroes in the graduating classes of thirty-two public high schools in eleven northern and western states showed that while Negroes comprised about 35 per cent of the total, only about 2 per cent of them were represented in the academically highest quarter of their various classes. This reflects a difference not only in socio-economic status, but in motivation and general cultural environment. The gap closes here at a grudging pace as well, and necessarily at a slower pace than the achievement of civil rights.

Housing discrimination, the key to physical integration, and the last, most resistant frontier of the civil rights revolution, is formally succumbing to that revolution. Old housing patterns change slowly at best; and there is the interim phenomenon of "tipping," the tendency of private open-occupancy developments to become preponderantly or wholly Negro. But, beyond that, even in a free and accepting market, residential patterns are normally wedded to social and economic patterns.

As whites move out of the central cities to satisfy—if nothing else—their socio-economic aspirations, the general socio-economic and educational levels of these cities drop. As Morton Grodzins points out, in an article included in this collection: "Many central cities of the great Metropolitan areas of the United States are fast becoming lower-class, largely Negro slums." The movement outward accelerates; the danger grows of statistical group differences becoming frozen. The "race-relations problem" becomes co-extensive with the national problems of urban life in general, and of growing social cleavage in general.

In sum, the problems of race relations are broader than the problems of discrimination which they include. It is now clear that the social objective all along was not just equal opportunity and desegregation but equal achievement and integration; and it is also clear that the former will not automatically—or perhaps swiftly enough—lead to the latter. Indeed the formula may have to be reversed under certain circumstances: extended individual opportunity may depend finally upon group achievement.

This is, hypothetically, the new frontier of race relations: to deal with those factors *other than discrimination* which seriously deter equal group achievement and integration. Such a frontier does not, of course, exist in any purity. The civil rights revolution is far from being completed. Discrimination in employment, housing and education is still a fact of life for the non-white population of the country. But the social remedies for discrimination are at hand and are, to varying degrees, being applied. It is the "post-bigotry" aspect of the problems—complicated by the continuing uses of bigotry—that has not been explored and that, in the long run, may prove most difficult to remedy.

The selections in this volume touch, for the most part, on these emerging "post-bigotry" problems.

SECTION ONE

Foreword: Ending the Past:
Equal Opportunity and Desegregation

EARL RAAB

One of the lesser accomplishments of the civil rights revolution has been to turn America into a vast laboratory for the study of social change. Deep cultural patterns are apparently being uprooted in an orderly and at least partly deliberate process. Society has been making calculated attempts to shape and accelerate the rough-hewn movements of history. Each turn of the road is marked by sharp fiat rather than by gentle voluntarism: a law is passed, a court decision is rendered, an administrative order is handed down, an economic boycott is launched. But social scientists, among others, have been reluctant to accept these dramatic engines of the civil rights revolution on face value, asking: Is it really working? By what process is it working? Is it leaving unreconciled pockets of resistant attitudes; by-passing or even aggravating problems of intergroup conflict? Two concepts have come to dominate the answers:

1.) If patterns of discrimination and segregation are altered, the attitudes and even the ideologies that seemed to create and support those patterns will also be altered.

The surface premise of civil rights legislation is that men's behavior can be regulated even if their attitudes cannot be. However, the inner premise holds that when behavior patterns are regulated, attitudinal patterns will also reshape themselves. The underlying assumption is

23

that the broad fabric of prejudice—behavior and attitude —is woven more of social habit than of individual pathology. These are generalizations so sweeping that numerous exceptions and complications are to be expected; but in their main sweep, these generalizations are supported by a growing body of evidence.

2.) American communities—North and South—will alter their discriminatory behavior if they are forced to make a clear choice between their commitments to discrimination and segregation, and their aspirations for economic advancement, peace and order, or education for their children.

In brief, people will tend to change their behavior towards Negroes, without initially changing their attitudes towards Negroes, if highly cherished values are at stake. As Melvin Tumin puts it, "between private feeling and public action there is room for the play of other factors which significantly influence the extent to which feeling will be translated into matching action or will be repressed on behalf of other values."* This framework of "other values" which might repress private feeling, Tumin refers to as *"countervailing perspectives . . .* [which] develop without any necessary or matching reduction in the emotional sets against which they are posed." In one study in a Southern community, he found that resistance to desegregation diminished as the situation moved from a "thinking" to a "doing" stage. When plans of action were proposed which called for closing down the schools or mobilizing for violent resistance, an awareness of consequences began to temper responses. Formal education did not seem to reduce prejudice towards Negroes, but, by

* Melvin Tumin, Paul Barton and Bernard Burnus, "Education, Prejudice and Discrimination: A Study in Readiness for Desegregation," *American Sociological Review,* February 1958, p. 41

enlarging value perspectives, did increase readiness for desegregation. College graduates held no less prejudiced an image of the Negro than did grammar school graduates, but, bringing "countervailing perspectives" to bear earlier, were less resistant to desegregation.

Indeed, this kind of "brinkmanship" is evident in patterns of Southern resistance to desegregation. Every evasive technique is tried. But in the final moment, when the choice is between desegregation and violent lawlessness or destruction of the school system, each community typically moves back a step. This happened in Norfolk, after "massive resistance" legal schemes failed in the courts. It happened in Little Rock and New Orleans after world-publicized mob-riot scenes, which, after all, involved only a handful of participants. It happened in Atlanta, which anticipated the consequences and desegregated peacefully on court order. At stake were not only community peace and community education, but the Southern drive for industrial expansion and new prosperity.

A rough formula for social change seems to lie in these two propositions which suggest that, even where attitudes are unsympathetic, desegregation and conditions of equal opportunity can be directly imposed, if the margin for evasion is removed; and that, once imposed, the changed patterns of community behavior will begin to change attitudes. In this way will public opinion peacefully remold itself to the historical American consensus on equal rights for all men.

A formula—even a partially validated one—is of little comfort to current generations of American non-whites whose goals are, by and large, personal rather than historical. Commissions that have studied the effects of fair employment laws on employment patterns report demonstrable progress. Massachusetts reported that "literally thousands of jobs, for the first time, have been opened to representatives of minority groups." But many more thousands of vacancies—if fewer each year—continue to be quietly filled on a discriminatory basis. Of the seventeen Southern states in which segregated schools were mandatory six years ago, only three now have no desegregated schools. But in at least twelve of those states, desegregation is piecemeal and token. In four of those "desegregated" states, in the spring of 1960, there were a total of 400 Negroes in desegregated schools. The year before there had been 199. In many areas, especially rural areas, no beginning has been made at all.

Some critics have noted these lagging conditions to argue that more reliance must be laid on voluntarism and formal educational processes. But if the basic formula for change is valid, the problem is one of pace, not of means; it is not the formula that is at fault but the failure to apply it more strenuously. The high anger characteristic of the American Negro community today, despite the fact that conditions are better rather than worse, is not just a product of rising aspirations; it also results from a sense that there is a remedial formula available which is not being fully used. "Gradualism," according to this view, is not just callous with respect to present generations, but misses the point entirely: in many cases *nothing* will happen, where there is resistance, unless the coercive tension is maintained at its highest possible pitch. This would mean, for example, government initiating hundreds of simultaneous law suits in local district courts to break down the barriers of segregation; Congress has refused to give the Attorney General's Office such authority. Freedom Riders, Freedom Sitters, and Freedom Bathers have attempted to pursue this stratagem in other areas of community life. The premise is that if the communities in question are pressed to the point where there is no legal alternative to desegregation, they will accede to it, and then gradually come to accept it.

In any case, with respect to the limited goals of desegregation and equal opportunity, the methodology is already indicated; only the speed is in question.

In "The Prejudiced Society," Raab and Lipset review much of the research literature that indicates that once desegregated and non-discriminatory conditions have been established—willingly or unwillingly—attitudes and emotions will reform themselves in the crucible of those new conditions.

In "Changing Social Roles in the New South," Joseph S. Himes describes some of the new conditions in the South which are conducive to the development of "countervailing perspectives" and of desegregation in general.

In "The Sit-Ins and the New Negro Student," Charles U. Smith comments on a new "identity" for Southern Negroes, which points up the growing readiness for desegregation of the Southern Negro community, as well as its growing insistence that the underlying formula of the civil rights revolution be played out more swiftly to its ultimate end.

The Prejudiced Society

EARL RAAB AND SEYMOUR MARTIN LIPSET

The problem of prejudice, as it presents itself to society, consists of overt acts which deny equal status or opportunity to people because of their racial, religious or ethnic identity. However, "prejudice" is often used in a specialized sense to describe an individual's state of mind or attitude. There has long been a popular tendency to reify "prejudiced attitude"; to conceive of it as a little mental package tucked away in a corner of the brain, waiting for the proper stimulus to bring it to life. According to this view, if a person has "a prejudiced attitude" against Filipinos, then when a Filipino brushes up against him, or enters the same room he's in, or applies to him for a job, or tries to move next door, this attitude would be triggered and the "prejudiced person" would act accordingly.

The evidence clearly indicates, however, that prejudiced attitudes are very far from being neat little mental packages; and that, at the very least, they do not predetermine prejudiced behavior.

Gordon Allport has partly defined an attitude as a "mental and neural state of readiness."[1] The meaningful reference here is to the fact that an attitude is a "mental and neural" state and not just to the fact that it is a state of readiness. A mechanical jack-in-the-box, crouched on its

[1] Gordon Allport, "Attitudes," in *A Handbook of Social Psychology*, edited by C. Murchison (Worcester: Clark University Press, 1935), p. 798

springs, might be said to have an attitude of readiness. Its attitude is such that it will jump up when the cover is removed. But a human attitude describes an internal state that has an independent existence, apart from any resultant behavior. If a child were simulating a jack-in-the-box in a school play, his attitude towards jumping out of the box in which he was crouched might consist of a combination of elements, e.g.: he may be displeased about the physical prospect of jumping out; on the other hand, he may have a strong fear of the derision he will face if he fails to jump. Both of these elements comprise his "attitude about jumping" at a given point. The attitude exists as a real fact even if the show is cancelled and he never does have the opportunity of jumping or not jumping.

Hostility and Stereotype

It is common to think of the prejudiced attitude as consisting of both hostility and an over-generalization or stereotype. It is even common to think of the hostility as flowing from the stereotype. But, in fact, it is possible for an individual to have the stereotype without the hostility, or the hostility without the stereotype. It is possible to cloak two groups with the same stereotype, and have different feelings about them. Saenger and Flowerman questioned some 450 college students as to their feeling of dislike for a number of human groups. They also asked these students to indicate the characteristics which they believed marked these groups. Presumably their likes or dislikes would be based on the kinds of characteristics which they attributed to these groups. This was not the case. Students who expressed a dislike for Jews ascribed to them characteristics which they also ascribed to other groups for whom they did *not* express a dislike. For example, 31 per cent of the students complained that the Jews were mercenary; but 24 per cent of them complained that Americans were mercenary and 38 per cent that businessmen were mercenary. However, Jews were more often disliked for this quality than were Americans or businessmen.

In a study made by B. M. Kramer, he marked off five "distance zones" from an area in which Negroes were moving and interviewed white residents in each of the zones. Zone 1 was the closest to this area of expanding Negro movement. Zone 5 was the most remote, three miles away. There was a general desire among white residents in all five zones to exclude Negroes from their neighborhoods. Kramer checked the stereotypes held by these white residents about Negroes, e.g., that Negroes were personally unclean or diseased. In Zone 1, where the white residents had the closest contact with the Negroes, only 5 per cent offered such stereotypes as reasons for exclusion; as against 25 per cent of the residents in Zone 5. However, the intensity of hostility in Zone 1 was higher than in Zone 5; in Zone 1, 64 per cent of the residents made spontaneous expressions of hostility, as against only 4 per cent in Zone 5. Whatever else may have been involved in the situation, it was clear that hostility and stereotype were not tied to each other.

A negative stereotype may exist without hostility; hostility without a negative stereotype; a combination of both cognitive and emotional elements may exist with varying degrees of intensity and with varying targets. A prejudiced attitude is indeed not a homogeneous mental package. Prejudiced attitude #1 is different from prejudiced attitude #2, and there is almost an endless variety of possibilities.

Frame of Reference—The Situational Factor

Not only do prejudiced attitudes differ widely from one individual to another, but they tend to differ from one situation to another for any given individual. For an attitude is not a thing, it is a process; it is an interaction. It is an interaction involving not only the person and the object, but all other factors that are present in any situation. A crude illustration: In his own home town, Jones may have the deepest contempt for Smith, who lives up the block. He considers Smith a rough character with bad manners and worse taste, socially unacceptable and intellectually barren. Jones has a *feeling* of distaste when he thinks of Smith, and avoids him conscientiously. It happens that Jones, alone on an unguided world tour, has a transportation breakdown in a primitive village in a backward country. The villagers are unfriendly, unlettered and unsanitary. Into this unhappy and improbable scene, after a couple of days, rides Smith. Jones may well greet him with a joyful embrace, rather than with distaste. His image of Smith as a boor may be replaced by the image of a man who at least has the good sense to speak English and to wash his hands before eating. Whether or not this feeling and image will carry over in any way when the two men return to their home town is another matter—but the fact remains that a different external situation has evoked a different attitude.

Sherif and Cantril have called this situational factor "frame of reference." They write:

> "The term 'frame of reference' is simply used to denote the functionally related factors (present and past) which operate at the moment to determine the particular properties of a psychological phenomenon (such as perception, judgment, affectivity)."

In psychological literature, the critical importance of the situational factor is supported by experiments on many levels. Wever and Zener had subjects judge the weight of a series of objects as "light" or "heavy." When the series of objects was changed from a light series to a heavy series, the same object that was formerly judged heavy was now perceived as light. McGarvey had her subjects rate the "social prestige" of various occupations and found that the desirability of any given occupation was dependent on the kind of occupational series with which it appeared.

Many research roads lead to the understanding that prejudiced attitudes can be highly situational in character. One evening at a summer camp, 30 young men were tested as to their attitudes towards Japanese-Americans. Following this, they were scheduled to attend a show at a local theatre. Instead, their show-going was cancelled, and they were forced to accomplish a series of complicated tasks. The same night, following the tasks, their attitudes towards Japanese-Americans were retested, and were found to be less favorable than they had been earlier in the evening. Nothing had changed in the interim with respect to the young men vis-a-vis Japanese-Americans, but some other factors in the situation had changed.

Deitrich Reitzes examined a situation, in which a group of white people had favorable attitudes towards Negroes at work and in shopping centers, but had unfavorable attitudes towards them living in their residential neighborhood. He traced these inconsistencies to different attitudinal "fields"; that is, each of these situations had different external forces operating to form the interaction of attitude. The unions to which the white people belonged were actively committed to intergroup equality at work. The Chamber of Commerce and business groups in the area involved were actively seeking Negro trade. The neighborhood civic club, however, was actively exclusionist. There were different "collective interests" involved in the different situations. In short, an individual does not typically have "an attitude" towards Negroes; he has many different attitudes depending on the circumstances.

There are a number of different ways in which this "situational" character of prejudice may be described:

A general attitude, about Negroes, for example, does not predetermine specific attitudes about Negroes. In other words, if a person has a general stereotype of Negroes, and a general hostility towards Negroes, this does not automatically mean that he will have an unfavorable attitude towards working in the same factory with Negroes.

One specific attitude towards Negroes, e.g., working with them, may have a quite different texture from another specific attitude, e.g., living next to them.

The same person may have one attitude about working next to Negroes in one situation, and a different attitude about working next to them in another situation.

In sum, a prejudiced attitude may shift from one moment and situation to another.

Disparity Between the Attitude and the Act

The situational nature of prejudice is evident, too, in the mass of evidence concerning the disparity between *expressed* attitudes and behavior.

A Chinese couple traveled twice across the United States, and up and down the Pacific Coast. During the course of this trip, they asked for service in hundreds of hotels, auto camps, tourist homes and restaurants. They were refused accommodations in only one sleeping place, and in none of the eating places. Six months after their trip, R. T. LaPiere sent a mail questionnaire to each of these places asking if Chinese could be accommodated. Over 90 per cent of the 47 sleeping places and of the 81 eating places that replied said that Chinese would *not* be accommodated.

In a Northeastern suburban community, three young women, two white and one Negro, entered 11 restaurants. They encountered no problems, and received nothing less than exemplary service. Two weeks later a letter was sent to the same restaurants asking for reservations for a similar group. There was no answer to the letters, and great resistance to the follow-up phone calls.

Saenger and Gilbert studied customer reactions to the employment of Negro sales personnel in New York City department stores. One group they interrogated had been observed as customers in stores where there were both Negro and white clerks. Twenty per cent of those who had bought from Negro clerks said they would disapprove of the policy of employing Negro clerks in the department stores; 21 per cent of those who had bought from white clerks expressed the same attitude. In other words, prejudice towards Negro clerks did not cause customers to avoid them in the stores. Over 40 per cent of those who said they would not buy in a store with Negro clerks had actually been observed not only in such a store but at a counter where there was a Negro clerk. One-third of those who said they would never buy from a Negro clerk had been observed buying from a Negro clerk less than an hour before they were interviewed.

The Behavior—Not the Attitude

It is true, of course, that the *expression* of an attitude may be different from, or at least only a surface part of an attitude. A person who is asked whether he would have any objection to rooming with someone of another racial extraction may honestly say, and honestly believe, that he is free of such prejudiced attitudes. But he may find, to his own shock, that when it comes down to it, he does have internal resistance to such a relationship; or indeed, without realizing it himself, he may find reasons and devices for avoiding such a relationship. Likewise, he may say that he *does* have objections, and when it comes down to it, he may not have these objections, or may not find them operative. His initial response may depend on the circumstances: who asks him and where. His ultimate reaction may also depend on the circumstances. This disparity between attitude as expressed and as it ultimately affects behavior merely re-emphasizes the *situational* character of the whole complex of prejudice. And it is the act of prejudice, not the attitude itself, which is the social problem of prejudice as earlier defined.

Andrew Kapos surveyed the attitudes of 30 segregated white gentile fraternities at the University of Michigan in 1953. He found a more intensive feeling of general prejudice against Jews than against Negroes. But he also found more willingness to admit Jews than Negroes to the fraternities, possibly because of the group standards which the fraternity members felt existed in the world around them. The attitudes of almost a thousand Texas manufacturers towards Negroes were tested; and the results were compared with the actual hiring practices of these manufacturers. It was found that the general attitude of a man towards Negroes had little to do with whether or not he employed them. An employer's willingness to hire Negroes was not significantly related to the degree of general hostility he felt or expressed towards Negroes.

In Panama there are places where one side of a street falls in the American Canal Zone, and the other side of the same street falls in Panamanian territory. Biesanz and Smith found that Panamanian Negroes tend to conform to discriminatory practices when they go to the Zone side of the street; while white Americans tend to adjust to non-discriminatory practices when they go to the Panamanian side.

Whether in the fraternities of Ann Arbor, the factories of Texas, or the streets of Panama, it is not the prejudiced attitude which is itself important to the social problem of prejudice. It is the act of excluding Negroes from the fra-

ternities and from the factories that makes prejudice a
problem for society. The attitudes are important to that
problem only insofar as they *cause* these acts. It is clear,
however, that a prejudiced attitude is not a kind of push-
button, nor a constant psychic bundle; it is, more accurately, an interaction in any given situation. It is clear that
general attitudes of prejudice do not necessarily predetermine prejudiced behavior; it is clear that a specific attitude
at one moment does not predetermine the act that will
eventuate at another moment. What, then, *is* the relationship between attitudes and behavior?

LEARNING PREJUDICE

*Prejudiced behavior typically shapes and alters prejudiced
attitudes. The learning of prejudice is affected primarily by
the kinds of social situations in which people live.*

The fact that attitudes do not necessarily predetermine
behavior, does not mean that attitudes and behavior do not
typically accompany each other. The human being is not a
mechanical jack-in-the-box. We do normally have feelings
and conceptions that accompany our behavior. But our
feelings and conceptions—our attitudes—do not necessarily
precede our behavior. The attitude of the boy who is going
to jump out of the box in the school play may be altered
by the very fact that he is going to jump out of the box;
just as his attitude immediately after his act may be shaped
by the bare fact that he did jump out.

In brief, behavior typically shapes and alters attitudes.
Cantril examined attitude polls on the subject of "lend-
lease" assistance to the Allies before the United States was
involved in World War II. He found that immediately
after Congress actually passed lend-lease legislation, attitudes toward such legislation became more favorable by

about 10 per cent. The point, according to Cantril is that public opinion tends to follow accomplished fact.

Stouffer and his associates asked white soldiers: How would you like it if your division had companies which included both Negro and white platoons? Seven per cent of those who already were in a company with Negro platoons replied that they disliked the situation; 20 per cent of those questioned who were in the same regiment but not in the same company as Negro platoons replied that they would dislike it; 24 per cent of those who were in the same division but not the same regiment as Negro platoons replied that they would dislike it; 62 per cent of those questioned who were not even in the same division as Negro platoons replied that they would dislike it. The further they were from the accomplished fact, the more they disliked it.

Deutsch and Collins surveyed attitudes of white residents in four different public housing projects in New York. In two, Negro and white families were assigned indiscriminately to the same apartment buildings. In the other two, Negroes were assigned to different buildings within the same project.

In all cases, the assignments were made under an automatic procedure that did not take into account the preference of those assigned. Asked if they would dislike living in the same buildings with Negroes, about three-quarters of the white respondents in the segregated projects said they would, as against only about one-quarter of those already living in the fully integrated units. About 50 per cent of those in the integrated projects said they desired to be friendly with their Negro neighbors, as against only about 10 per cent in the segregated projects. General attitudes towards Negroes seemed to be affected as well: about 75 per cent of those in the integrated units said they respected Negroes in general, as against well below 50 per cent of those in the segregated projects.

The Prejudiced Society

Attitudes After the Fact

Many research studies show that specific attitudes change after the fact, e.g.: attitudes towards living in the same neighborhood, serving in the same Army company. These studies are evidence that specific attitudes do shape themselves to specific behavior. However these studies do *not* indicate that a shift in one specific attitude towards a minority group will necessarily affect other specific attitudes towards the same group; or that a shift in a specific attitude will always affect the expression of a general attitude as it apparently did in the Deutsch and Collins study.

Harding and Hogrefe studied the attitudes of white employees towards Negro co-workers in department stores. The white employees were divided into three groups according to the nature and extent of their contact with Negroes. Group I included those who had worked in departments where there had been at least one Negro whose job was on an equal or superior plane. Group II included those who had worked in departments where Negroes had been of lower working status than themselves. Those in Group III had never worked in a department with Negroes.

They were all asked: "How would you feel about taking a new job in which there were both Negroes and white people doing the same kind of work as you?" Seventy-three per cent of Group I, 61 per cent of Group II, and 48 per cent of Group III said they would be favorable. But there was no significant difference between the three groups when they were asked, for example, whether they would want to sit next to Negroes on the bus or train. The experience of working with Negroes apparently only produced a more favorable attitude towards Negroes in that specific "fellow-employee" frame of reference.

A further clue may be found in the study of Daniel Wilner and his associates of attitudes of white residents in public housing projects. This three-year study compared two kinds of white tenants: those who lived close to Negroes and those who lived at a relative distance. In neither case was the distance a matter of choice for the white residents who had been assigned to their quarters in these public projects. As in the Deutsch-Collins study, it was discovered that attitudes changed favorably as the distance to the Negroes decreased. Not only was there a significant difference in the specific attitude (i.e., living near Negroes), but again an apparent shift in general attitudes. In one project, for example, where Negroes and whites lived in the same buildings, 53 per cent of the respondents said that they generally liked and respected Negroes; in another project where the buildings were all-white and all-Negro, only 36 per cent of the respondents said that they generally liked and respected Negroes.

However, the Wilner study went further. Among one group of women who lived close to Negroes, 32 per cent who had no personal contact with their Negro neighbors beyond casual greetings, had a high degree of general esteem for Negroes; 45 per cent who, in addition, had extended street conversation with their Negro neighbors had a high degree of general esteem for Negroes; and 74 per cent who had neighborly associations with Negroes, i.e., behaved like neighbors, had a high degree of esteem generally for Negroes.

Proximity was not a matter of choice but of automatic assignment. The greater the proximity, the more likely was there to be neighbor-like activity. A point made by the Wilner study is that the shift in general attitudes came not so much from mere contact or proximity, but from a changed pattern of behavior. The white residents who *acted* like neighbors came most often to *feel* like neighbors on many levels.

I. N. Brophy found a very marked reduction in general anti-Negro prejudice among white merchant seamen who, without the benefit of choice, had worked with Negro sailors. Thirty-three per cent of those who had never shipped with Negroes were rated as unprejudiced; 46 per cent of those who had shipped with Negroes once; 62 per cent who had shipped with Negroes twice; and 82 per cent of those who had shipped with Negroes five or more times were rated as unprejudiced. This was in sharp contrast to the Harding and Hogrefe study of the limited shifts in general attitudes for whites who had worked with Negroes in department stores. But these seamen not only worked together very closely, but also lived together 24 hours a day. And neighborly relationships are, of course, more general and encompassing than working relationships.

Behavior Shapes Attitude

In other words, evidence indicates that specific attitudes shape themselves to behavior. People who actually work with Negroes, especially as equals, develop attitudes favorable towards working with Negroes. People who actually are neighbors of Negroes develop attitudes favorable towards being neighbors of Negroes. Evidence also indicates that general attitudes shape themselves to behavior only if that behavior is itself general in nature. People who behave towards Negroes as full equals on every level tend to develop attitudes toward them as full equals on every level.

Thus, the mass of modern evidence runs counter to the "attitudes-first" fallacy, which holds that prejudice is a lurking state of mind that spills over into overt behavior. It might be more accurate to say that the prejudiced state of mind is typically a function of behavior; except for the danger that *this* formula might be over-simplified into a kind of reverse fallacy. Actually, there emerges an understanding that the key to prejudice must be found *outside* the realm of attitude-behavior relationships. The evidence has demonstrated how both attitudes and behavior are affected by the social frame of reference in which they occur.

In an integrated housing situation, attitudes and behavior are different than in a segregated housing situation. In an integrated army situation, attitudes and behavior are different than in a segregated army situation. In a shopping center situation attitudes and behavior towards Negroes are different than in a neighborhood situation. On one side of a Panamanian street, a white man's behavior towards Negroes may be different than on the other side of the street. It is this *situational* factor which is central to both attitude and behavior; which can stand outside any behavior-attitude spiral and avoid the fruitless question: "Which comes first?"

The effect of the situational factor on the social problem of prejudice can be found in the dramatic story of post-war integration in the armed forces. A military installation comprises a kind of community in itself, with its own community practices and patterns. Soldiers, sailors, marines and airmen for the most part live as well as work within the military setting. Traditionally, the armed forces community had followed the racial patterns of the nation's lowest common denominator: the deep South. The assumption was made that only in this way could the armed forces accommodate the young men from the South as well as from other parts of the country who entered the services with deep-set attitudes of prejudice. Segregation was the rule on almost every level. Most military leaders expected it to stay that way indefinitely. In 1948, however, an edict was handed down by administrative order from President

Truman's office: the armed forces were to be thoroughly and effectively integrated.

In its own inimitable way, the armed forces implemented this edict by a series of direct military orders. Today, there is effective integration throughout all the branches of service. In 1953, in an extensive survey of the effects of the desegregation edict five years after it was issued, Lee Nichols was able to report that Negroes and whites, from all parts of the country were not just training and fighting together, but were also eating at the same tables, sleeping in the same quarters, drinking beer together, going to church and the movies together.

Beyond the Call of Duty

A typical illustration of the process has been provided by Brigadier General Frank McConnell who had been assigned, shortly after the integration edict, to command a major training base in South Carolina. Customarily, as the recruits poured in, the Negroes were separated from the whites and established in separate organizations. General McConnell issued an order that the next 55 draftees who arrived would comprise a platoon, regardless of their color, and that this procedure would be followed with all subsequent arrivals. The order was issued verbally and "that," he said "was the end of segregation in Fort Jackson." There were no interracial incidents then or thereafter.

"I would see recruits, Negro and white, walking down the street, all buddying together," said the General. "The attitude of the Southern soldiers was that this was the Army way; they accepted it the same way they accepted getting booted out of bed at 5:30 in the morning."

This was the Army way. This was the new social situation, the new set of practices which surrounded the white soldier who had been accustomed to quite another way of life. His new community accepted it, he accepted it. There were no incidents of any consequence. Scattered grumbling that was heard when the policy was announced, but before it was implemented, disappeared when integration actually took place. Apprehension had been unwarranted. A Congressional committee reported that "the almost total absence of opposition that had been anticipated in the enlisted men is a contributing factor in the success of this policy. The men were more ready for equality of treatment than the officer corps had realized." Commanders reported that interracial incidents had *lessened* under the policy of integration, as a result of the lessening of tensions.

The servicemen did not necessarily retain these specific attitudes or behavior patterns when they returned to their home towns: The situational factors had shifted back again. In many cases, their *general* attitudes may have altered somewhat, at least temporarily, because of their total-living experiences in integration; and the aspiration levels of the Negro servicemen may also have been raised as a result. But they settled back without difficulty in the segregated patterns of their home communities. More definitively, the practices of the armed forces had a direct impact on certain practices in the non-military community. Negro and white soldiers sat side by side on a city bus in Columbia, South Carolina, where such mingling was actually prohibited by law. Restaurants near military posts decided to admit Negroes along with white soldiers, partly because white and Negro soldiers began to accompany each other in town. In Amarillo, Texas, the USO club was opened to Negro airmen for the first time. Amarillo University began to admit Negroes to its extension classes, George L. P. Weaver, formerly of the CIO, told Lee Nichols that the elimination of segregation in the armed forces opened new job opportunities for Negroes with government contractors; indeed in the integrated military, Negro servicemen were

44

often able to learn vocational skills which they otherwise could have had no opportunity to learn.

At the very least, within the relatively uncomplicated society bounded by the armed forces, the *social problem* of prejudice had been virtually eliminated by the outlawing of prejudiced practices. Equality of opportunity is in effect. The aspirations of the non-whites within the military setting are being met. Interracial "incidents" and tensions have been reduced. This is not really being enforced at bayonet point, but has come to be accepted by servicemen. In terms of attitudes, they have, by and large, responded "beyond the call of duty," in their fraternization with fellow-servicemen of another race. Not only has behavior changed, which is the crux of the social problem, but behavior has patently shaped attitudes.

The Situation or The Personality

Perhaps then the most effective and workable approach to understanding the phenomenon of prejudice is through an investigation of the kinds of *social situations* which give rise to and sustain prejudiced behavior and attitudes. This is a sharply different approach from that which would investigate what kinds of *people* are prone to prejudice.

This is not to underestimate the special validity of an approach to prejudice from the vantage point of personality and personality differences. There are good reasons for making such a psychological approach. Prejudice serves an emotional function for many people. It helps them to shift blame from themselves to others, to rationalize their aggressions, or otherwise provides an outlet for their special emotional needs. Some people with special emotional needs have a special susceptibility to prejudice. In attempting to understand or remedy the particular virulence or persistence of a given individual's prejudice, it is often necessary to understand his psychological history.

One white factory worker got along very well with his co-worker who happened to be Negro. They were friendly, ate their lunches together, worked together harmoniously. Suddenly the white worker began to have severe marital troubles and seemed headed towards a divorce. He began to make slurring references to the Negro's race and they finally had to be separated. Another man, bitter because he was making no progress in his business firm, blamed the "Jews" in top management and became vocally anti-Semitic, although it turned out that there weren't any Jews in the management of the firm. One study of veterans found that those who were generally frustrated and felt that they had been subject to "bad breaks" in the service were more often prejudiced than those who felt they had experienced "good breaks" in the service. There is evidence that many of those who stigmatize the Negro as hypersexual are indeed guilt-ridden by their own sexuality, and are attempting to rid themselves of that guilt by projecting it onto the Negro.

The body of psychological knowledge which throws light on these reactions is extremely helpful in explaining individual differences and in helping to treat individual problems. Since certain emotional needs are universal, in one degree or another, this knowledge even helps to explain the special "attractiveness" that prejudice seems to have for human beings in general.

But it does not explain the specific *social problem* of prejudice with which our society is currently burdened. Presumably the factory worker who was having trouble with his wife would have found *some* scapegoat, even if there were no Negro available. It might have been the thinnest man in the factory, or the fattest, or the one with red hair, or perhaps just the one with whom he was most incompatible. The need to blame other people instead of one-self; irrelevantly to work out on other people one's guilt or aggressiveness or fear is an unhealthy condition in itself. It is a problem in mental health. Those who have this problem are undoubtedly more susceptible to prejudice and to other social aberrations than those who do not have such a problem. But this condition itself does not create the specific social evils attending prejudice as described earlier. It is only when these problems are displaced on groups and help establish a deep-going pattern of denying equal opportunity to specific groups that the social problem of prejudice emerges. In short, the factory worker's psychological reaction does not create the social problem of prejudice, it merely operates within the social framework of a pattern of prejudice which already exists.

Furthermore, the psychological approach, as valuable as it is, does not explain the preponderance of people who engage in prejudiced behavior, but do *not* have special emotional problems. It does not explain the widespread pattern of prejudice. It does not explain why prejudice is more intense in one place and time than in another.

The Lessons of Social Situations

These aspects of the social problem of prejudice are explainable only in terms of our *learning* prejudice much as we learn our other basic patterns of social behavior. But people do not typically learn their social values and social behavior in the same way that they learn the arithmetic table. It is not a matter of formal training or mere intellectual acceptance. A child may "learn" the social precept that it is wrong to steal, but may steal nonetheless. He has effectively learned the social value of honesty only to the extent that he has "internalized" that value; i.e., to the extent that this social value has become a natural and unthinking part of his behavior. It is not that he weighs consequences, but that it would "go against his grain" to steal.

This is not the kind of learning which basically is effected in the classroom, or even at the mother's knee. It is shaped fundamentally not by lecture or exhortation, but, in a kind of "creeping socialization," by the kinds of social situations in which people live, and, especially, in which they grow up.

It then becomes necessary to define more precisely the nature of "social situation" as it applies to prejudice; and to discover the kinds of social situations which give rise to and sustain prejudice.

THE PREJUDICED COMMUNITY

The pattern of community practices is the fountainhead of prejudice: of prejudiced behavior and of prejudiced attitudes.

The growing child learns his social behavior primarily by following the modes and models of behavior around him. Indeed, he has little choice. He learns how to behave towards people of other racial and religious groups by seeing how other people behave, and by automatically participating in the behavior patterns which already exist.

Consider the extreme but not atypical case of a community where the Negro population has been traditionally subordinate on every level. The Negro with whom the young child comes into contact is a domestic in his home; or an elevator operator or janitor or a worker in some other menial capacity. The Negroes he knows are not as well educated as the white people he knows, nor as well dressed, nor as well housed. The white people in his community do not socialize with Negroes, nor share the same public accommodations with them. No Negroes sit down at the same dinner table with him or with the people he knows; Negroes are not customers in the restaurants or hotels to which he is taken. Negroes are addressed by their first name, but always address the white people as "Mr." or "Mrs." They do not go to the same school as white children. They sit in separate sections of the bus. They use different rest rooms in the bus stations. If there is a tight fit on the sidewalk, it is the Negro pedestrian who gives way.

These are the social situations, i.e., the overt sets of relationships with which the child is surrounded. He does not have to be *told* that Negroes are "inferior," or what his relationships to them are supposed to be. These are apparent. Even more important, he is part of the white community and necessarily he *behaves* within the framework of these existing relationships. It is not just that his parents use a different rest room than do the Negroes. *He* uses a different rest room than the Negroes. *He* sits in the white section of the bus. *He* behaves towards them as social inferiors, and naturally comes to accept them as social inferiors. It isn't necessary to inculcate in him explicit attitudes about the social inferiority of Negroes. More likely, it is necessary for him to develop attitudes that do not conflict with his behavior.

Negroes conform to the prevailing patterns in such a community not only because they must, but also in part because they have accepted the values of the dominant community, and for the same reasons. They have been part of the same behavior patterns.

This process takes place at an early age. In one nursery school study, when pre-school Negro children were given a white and Negro doll to play with, they almost uniformly preferred the white doll.

Schools for Prejudice

There is a tendency to believe that these kinds of prejudicial behavior patterns are to be found preponderantly in the deep South. It is often startling to those in the northern and western parts of the country to find, by the most casual self-survey, the extent to which their own communities are "schools for prejudice" by dint of similar ongoing situations.

In the North and West, Negroes and whites typically live in different neighborhoods. That these Negro neighborhoods are usually inferior to the white is a fact readily apparent to the young observer. The proportion of substandard housing occupied by Negroes in 1952, according to U. S. Census standards, was six times as great as that occupied by whites. This was a uniform condition around the country. Nor is residential separatism restricted to the racial level. The Anti-Defamation League found, in a 1959 survey, that housing segregation on a religious basis was becoming more prevalent than was thought to be the case. For example, it found that a number of residential communities in the Chicago area were almost completely closed to Jews, and others had "large areas where Jews are barred."

Negroes typically work in lower-status jobs in communities throughout the nation. An index of this comparative status is the fact that the average earnings of the Negro worker is little more than half that of the white worker. This is partly the result of the history of educational and economic disadvantage which is the heritage of the Negro. But it is to a large extent the result of current prejudice. Where surveys have been made of job orders by employers in the North and West, in communities as widely separated as Los Angeles and Chicago, it has been found that at least 75 per cent of the job orders for white collar workers specify "white only." At least 25 per cent of these job orders specify "Christian only." (In 1959, the State of California took steps to remedy this situation with the passage of a Fair Employment Practices Act.)

It has been estimated that about one-quarter of the Negro school children *outside* the South go to schools that are in fact substantially all-Negro, and about half go to schools where there is only token mixing. This is largely a result of segregated housing patterns.

John P. Dean supervised a study of 248 cities, ranging in population from 10 thousand to 500 thousand, to determine the extent to which American Jews were thoroughly integrated. Three tests were used: admission to Junior League; admission to country clubs and city clubs; admission to exclusive residential areas. In one-third of the cities, Jews are denied admission to all three. In only 20 out of the 248 cities are some Jews accepted in all three, and these 20 are smaller cities. In more than half of the 50 largest cities in the study, Jews are denied admission to all three categories; and in only one are they admitted to all three.

These behavior patterns are not only the substance of prejudice as a social problem; they are also the breeding conditions of prejudice. In a very real sense, prejudiced behavior reproduces itself; carries within it its own seeds of continuity. In the same sense, prejudice is a dramatic example of the "self-fulfilling prophecy." The prejudiced image of a Negro as a constitutionally menial worker is sustained by the prejudiced behavior which in fact freezes him as a menial worker.

The Projection of Prejudice

The learning of prejudice is a natural result of actual participation in patterns of prejudiced behavior; or of first-hand observation of the patterns of prejudiced behavior in the community; but it may also result from *vicarious* participation, or *second-hand* observation of the patterns of prejudiced behavior. A society provides many "cues" for social behavior, e.g.: "white" and "colored" signs above public drinking fountains; or classified ads in the newspapers which read "gentile only"; or house-for-sale signs which read "white only" or "restricted."

In these several ways, then, it is on the level of actual behavior situations that the normal reproduction of prejudice is effected. It is within the framework of these behavior situations that individual differences, except perhaps the most pathological, operate. It is on the base of these behavior situations that the behavior-attitude spiral of prejudice builds. Attitudes and explicit ideologies are most firmly constructed on the foundation of these existing social situations.

Indeed, the attitudes which must develop to accompany human behavior are *implied* in this behavior and it is in this way that such attitudes are primarily learned rather than by direct instruction. By the time a child is told for the first time that "Negroes are inferior," he is already convinced of it. On the other hand, by the time he is told for the first time that "Negroes are *not* inferior" it is already often too late. He will resist the idea. Or, if he is finally intellectually convinced of the fact that Negroes are not inferior, he may evade the consequences. He may find some other reason for behaving towards the Negroes *as though* they were inferior. It is axiomatic in all learning situations that rhetorical exhortations have little chance of success when they are in battle against actual behavior patterns. For example, a child will not tend to be honest because his father tells him to be, if the same father is constantly engaged in dishonest practices himself.

Studies of the development of prejudice in children show

that young children who have not yet been involved in prejudiced behavior patterns, may pick up prejudiced talk, but this doesn't affect their unprejudiced behavior. Later, after having become involved in prejudiced behavior patterns, they may pick up democratic language in the schools or elsewhere, but this doesn't affect their prejudiced behavior. By the age of 15, Gordon Allport points out, "considerable skill is shown in imitating the adult pattern."[2]

They are now able to rationalize their prejudiced behavior whenever necessary and resort to the prejudiced ideologies which do not precede but follow prejudiced behavior patterns.

In brief, the pattern of *community practices* serves as the primary source of prejudice in behavior and attitude. This does not mean that we are merely back on the causative merry-go-round, where behavior chases attitude and attitude chases behavior in a dismally unending circle. "Community practices" connotes more than just the sum total of individual behavior at any given time. It means customary collective behavior. It means collective habits which tend to perpetuate themselves with their own momentum, such as the collective habit of smoking tobacco or drinking coffee.

Similarly, prejudiced community practices typically reproduce themselves by force of *custom*. All other things being equal, these practices are passed automatically from one generation to the next. John Dollard, after studying traditional patterns of prejudice in a Southern town, wrote:

> "The master defense against accurate social perception . . . is always . . . the tremendous conviction of rightness about any behavior form which exists. What is done is de facto right and is justified by the considera-

---

[2] Gordon W. Allport, *The Nature of Prejudice* (Cambridge: Addison-Wesley, 1954) p. 310.

tion that it has not been invented by current culture bearers but comes to them through sacred tradition."

The Persistence of Prejudice

The sheer power of custom recreates prejudiced community practices—which in turn, typically, breeds individual practices of prejudice, and, then, individual attitudes of prejudice. As a matter of fact, it is possible for prejudiced custom to persist without building up *any* corresponding attitudes.

For example, it has become commonplace for investigators of prejudiced employment practices to find the following kind of situation:

A personnel officer in a large firm tells a Jewish applicant, in effect, that he is sorry but the firm does not hire Jews as salesmen. A complaint is brought to the head of the firm, who expresses genuine astonishment. "What difference does it make?" he asks. "A good salesman is a good salesman." A visit is then made to the personnel officer who himself expresses genuine astonishment. No Jews had ever been hired by that firm, and he had just assumed that it was policy.

The department stores of a city with a fairly large Negro population had never hired a Negro clerk. As the store owners were approached on this situation, one by one, they indicated that they really had no objection to employing Negroes, and really hadn't given the matter much thought. It just "hasn't been done." One department store departed from the custom and hired Negro clerks; the others followed cheerfully and without incident.

These customary community practices, with or without corresponding attitudes, are the "frame of reference," the *situational* key to the prevention of and altering of the widespread phenomenon of prejudiced behavior and prejudiced attitudes. This pattern of community practices is the basic remedial target, rather than emotional maladjustment, or any given set of prejudiced attitudes. When this pattern of community practice changes—whether by law, direct action or otherwise; whether willingly or reluctantly —the prevailing pattern of community attitudes will be likely to change accordingly. Laws prohibiting the sale of liquor in the United States have dramatically failed to change attitudes about liquor; but these laws have failed to change community practices in the first place. There is impressive indication however, that in the area of social relationships, and specifically in the area of intergroup relationships, community practices *can* be changed prior to corresponding attitudinal changes, and will then serve to effect such attitudinal changes.

Changing Social Roles in the New South

JOSEPH S. HIMES

Some Institutional Changes in the South

Sociologists have captured and expressed the whole panorama of profound social change in the South by the concept of "the civilization process." This phenomenon refers to the progressive control of Southern people over both the physical and social environments by means of increasing rational and scientific understanding. The major regional correlates of the civilization process include extensive changes of social and economic relations, alterations of community organization, modifications of structures of class and race, and variations of traditional belief systems.

The proportion of rural population continues to decline as the urban percentage increases. At the same time an even greater proportion of the total population of the region is coming under the dominance of urban living. As a consequence, the demographic and ecological aspects of community structure are becoming steadily more urban in basic character. Associated with these changes are important transformations of the institutional structure of the region.

Industry is replacing agriculture at an accelerating rate as the major economic activity. In the urban industrial climate of social life, the previously informal understandings between workers and employers are giving way to for-

57

mal associational contracts. Many other formerly personal economic relations are becoming formal and explicit, illustrated in social security protection for superannuated household servants and agricultural workers, in installment contracts for time-payment purchases, and in voluntary payroll deductions for contributions and insurance premiums.

With the transition from agriculture to industry, control of the regional power structure moves from the "landed gentry" to the industrial owners. In the Atlantic and Gulf coastal states the balance of regional power is shifting from the rural tidewater section to the industrial piedmont areas. The reins of control are changing from the hands of the regionally old families to those of the new financiers and absentee corporations. Both the mood and the manner of control are losing the quality of intimacy and paternalism and are becoming rationalistic and impersonal.

Furthermore, the structure and control of the region's institutional apparatus are becoming increasingly centralized. This trend, under way for a number of years, is evident in industry and business, government, and voluntary organizations. Consider, for example, the establishment of state and regional branches of leading industrial corporations, chain stores, national labor unions, and transportation and communications systems. The trend is further evidenced in the spread to the South of national nonprofit service, welfare, and religious agencies. Centralization of institutional structure is also being achieved through reconciliation of ancient differences between Southern branches and some of the religious denominations throughout the rest of the nation.

The centrally organized and controlled state system of public education is an indigenous feature of the regional institutional structure. Compliance with provisions of the Social Security Act fostered centralization of state systems of public welfare. Moreover, the expansion of services of the federal government, the poverty of some local communities, and the growing demand for improved public facilities and services are further accentuating this trend toward centralization of political institutions.

These transformations of the regional institutional apparatus are exerting a telling influence upon the traditional Southern family. Far-reaching modifications of member roles and the manner of their systematization are in process. Family interests tend to become individualized, with the result that primary solidarity and intimate family relations are seriously weakened. The closely integrated, patriarchal, and stable rural family type is disappearing with the rise to dominance of the associational type of unstable, equalitarian urban family system. Meanwhile, family experience tends to reflect and to support the trends of change that issue from other phases of the region's institutional structure.

And, finally, there is the multi-sided attack upon racial segregation and discrimination. One major dimension of this phase of change is embodied, of course, in the series of federal court actions that culminated with the May 17, 1954, decision of the Supreme Court prohibiting public-school segregation. Many voluntary organizations and business concerns have abandoned the practice of racial segregation of their own accord. Alterations of the institutional structures of race relations appear to be tied up with the civilization process in the region.

Some Changing Social Roles

This broad matrix of institutional change is reflected in profound alteration of traditional social roles, i.e.: patterns of expected individual behavior. For example:

1. Attention has already been called to the dwindling

number, power, and prestige of the old credit merchants, the exploitative and paternalistic big farmers and mill-owners, and the regionally old and prestigious families. In the piedmont and inland cities there has emerged a small regionally aloof and powerful industrial owner-class. Many from this class are absentee owners, or at least latter-day fugitives from the South. This small group of owners and controllers functions within the national and international economic and social stratosphere, so to speak. They maintain economic ties with such financial centers as New York and Chicago and participate in the international social life of the Four Hundred at the famous wintering and watering spots of three continents. They exert economic, political, and social control in the region through sectionally prominent and well-known representatives.

The base of the changing Southern economy rests upon some new socio-economic types. Transformation of the region's inefficient one-crop system tends to favor a new type of agricultural worker and operator. There are still small-farm owners, tenants, and sharecroppers, but instead of their being continuously in debt to the credit merchant or the plantation commissary, they are mortgaged to the finance company for an expensive automobile, a television set, and a variety of kitchen and farm appliances of which their fathers never dreamed. When they run out of ready cash, they can seek work in a nearby industrial plant. They are consumers in the new mass market where newness is essential and where economic relations are impersonal and contractual.

Industrialization and urbanization are producing a new type of secular, rationalistic, and self-conscious worker. This new city worker is altering the class structure of the Southern city and the beliefs of the urban upper classes. He joins the new industrial labor unions. He is frequently in the new mass market, often on a time-payment basis, for a great variety of goods and services. He buys many new appliances for his home, the services of doctors and lawyers for his family, and even a college education for his children. His outlook on the world and his way of living are powerfully influenced by television, the time clock, the factory and machine, the pay check, labor-union ideology, and the modern city. He comes to conceive of himself as distinct from, and hostile to, his employer. He identifies himself with other workers in his union, his industry, and his station in life rather than with "Southern folks." This new industrial worker is isolated, crowd-minded, insecure, and aggressive, and is becoming accustomed to mass participation. He comprises the larger part of the television audience, the baseball crowd, the labor union, the independent voter, the bargain-day customer, the comic-strip reader, and the movie audience.

Issuing directly from economic change are two types of middle-class roles. The numerous new business and industrial establishments and their top managerial personnel exist and operate in a competitive and highly rationalized consumers' economy. This form of organization and operation was largely unknown to the old-style Southern businessman, planter, or trader, whose mercantile enterprise was based upon a surplus labor supply that was controlled by credit and impervious alike to the imperatives of efficiency and the preferences of local consumers. These new managers and technical personnel frequently are Northern city individuals by birth or by specialized training and outlook. They are more efficiency-minded, more specialized, and more rationally or scientifically oriented than their economic predecessors. Regarding their reaction to the region and its ways, N. J. Demerath says:

> While some seek to gain acceptance by conforming to the traditional political and social views of the conservative or reactionary whites, many of the new managers and owners are non-conformists. Many of them have

been sent to the South by their companies or by the government. They do not plan to stay indefinitely and are not greatly concerned about being accepted by the old Southern elites.[1]

It is reported in many localities that while they fail to sympathize with racial prejudice against the Negro, they tend to be anti-Semitic. In some Southern cities, members of the new middle class, either from necessity or by preference, establish their own "social set" and equip it with country club and the other apparatus of elegant living.

At the same time, the professional middle class has grown in size, independence, and outlook. Statistics show that the proportion of Southern workers engaged in tertiary —roughly middle class—occupations has been growing rapidly in recent years. The expanding professional middle class finds a rapidly growing market for its goods and services among the new working classes, urban or agricultural. And since members of this class now have a ready market among the new Southern workers for their skills and services, the new professional middle-class persons need no longer kowtow as the deferential servants of the old and declining upper-class families. In various ways, therefore, the white-collar classes are displaying an independence of tradition and control that was rare in the Southern city of the recent past.

2. Many circumstances point to the emergence of the "mass" type of individual in the "new South." In this connection, regional change has three crucial consequences. First, the individual, either urban or rural, is increasingly subjected to the national ubiquitous and pervasive process of mass communication. He tends more and more to live the traditional Southern way of life in the mass American

[1] "Desegregration Education and North Carolina," unpublished paper read at the annual meeting of the North Carolina Negro College Conference, Raleigh, November 16, 1955

manner. Second, the individual becomes more and more isolated from identification in the stable, inclusive primary groups and institutions of the old and disappearing sectional South. He emerges as a discrete, independent, rationalistic, and self-directed creature. And third, the new regional individual is beginning to participate directly as a rationalistic and self-conscious unit in the emerging mass patterns of social action. Whether farmer, industrial worker, middle-class person, or minority-group member, the new individual in the new South is growing independent, mass-minded, and capable of direct social action on a wide range of fronts.

Under these evolving circumstances, the individual must become capable of entering into many different and changing situations of mass experience. He therefore tends to develop a galaxy of novel segmental social roles, or specialized social functions. New status categories correspond to the significant features of the segmental roles. In this way individuals of whatever traditional station in life and cultural subgroup can be absorbed into the rapidly changing and indefinitely expansible mass social system.

There are appropriate names for the more common role-status configurations. In the new South, people speak of workers, fans, tourists, shoppers, spectators, readers, customers, voters, followers, consumers, subscribers, registrants, and so on. The term "fan," for instance, refers to a general status that includes all kinds of persons who wax enthusiastic about such features of mass culture as professional athletics, "hi fi," progressive jazz, or detective stories. Fans—of whatever variety—occupy a place and play a part in the new South that is characteristically different from that of workers, consumers, or tourists, say. Little essential distinction is drawn between the rich and the poor, the educated and the unlettered, the old and the young, or between men and women.

In the aggregate, the individuals who occupy these new categorical statuses and perform these new specialized roles comprise a new regional type. Creature and creator of change, regional mass man is more enveloped in the national social stratosphere than immersed in the regional substratum. This new role type is isolated, independent, specialized, directly active, and, above all, significantly American, rather than "Southern," in outlook.

3. Within this general context of regional change, the significance and features of the so-called "new Negro" become evident. With urbanization, change of the occupational structure, and alteration of the structure of racial relations, Negroes in substantial numbers are entering a world of widened individual experience and expectations. Such changes tend to accentuate the resentment against caste limitations by resistance and aggression. Racial militancy has become an esteemed group value. Its transmission, glorification, and inculcation are fostered by organized agencies. The National Association for the Advancement of Colored People and the Negro press are leaders in this new orientation. The Negroes in the ranks and leadership of labor unions, in responsible positions of government, attending classes in the universities of border and Southern states, and residing in homes in formerly segregated areas are exemplars of the new Negro. The traits that distinguish this role type, however, are in reality not new. The newness seems rather to inhere in the refusal to conceal, repress, or compromise the spirit of militancy and resistance that has characterized some Negroes in all stations throughout our national history. Traditionally only the leaders were militant. Frederick Douglass and W. E. B. DuBois are cases in point. The masses were oriented toward compromise and accommodation to the strictures of the racial caste system. Booker T. Washington is the symbol of this traditional orientation. In the ebb and flow

of racial change, the spirit of compromise and accommodation is being curtailed and the orientation toward militancy is being accentuated and glorified. Nowadays the personalities of ordinary Negroes include the traits of militancy, aggression, and resistance formerly restricted to the dramatic and celebrated leaders.

In the course of regional change Negroes have become heir to many (for them) new and different statuses and roles. The personalities that emerge from the shaping of behavior under such changing circumstances are in fact new. They symbolize and evidence the shifting areas of interracial contact and tension, since they reflect changes in the traditional pattern of ethnic caste stratification. In the space remaining it is possible to do nothing more than enumerate some of the manifestations and dimensions of this new regional role type.

With particular reference to the consequences of integration, Hylan Lewis and Mozell Hill have captured a significant dimension of newness in the emergent Negro middle class with the picturesque phrase "arrivestes." Thus they write:

Participation on a basis of merit means not only that a wider range of callings is open to Negroes but also that many Negroes are upgraded to higher skill classifications and to unique (to the Negro community) and more prestigious positions or colleague relationships. This new basis for ranking is reenforced by generally increased income which makes possible for new groups the indulgence of living and leisure-time tastes on levels—and thanks in part to desegregation—in places hithertofore not accessible. A premium tends to be placed on achievement and behavior that represent breaks with the offerings and norms of the meager and restricted Negro community. To the extent that this behavior is new and to the extent that significant other areas of life are still restricted or 'racial,' it and the *arrivestes* who practice it may have a feverish and exaggerated quality.[2]

In further analysis, Lewis and Hill identify a type of marginality that characterizes the new Negro. Of this dimension of personality they write:

> Segmental desegregation tends to produce a new type of marginal person. This person is in some ways a counterpart of the hybrid institution mentioned earlier that operates with reference to special or limited interests in both Negro and white communities. It is increasingly common for both Negroes and whites to play many pluralistic roles inside and outside the uneven color line. As individuals move more easily from partially or almost completely segregated to less or non-segregated orders, there need be no consistency in role or context in residential areas, school, church, assembly line, or store, business or profession, public office, leisure-time activities, intimate associates . . .[3]

In urban communities of the region Negroes in increasing numbers are being subjected to the mass processes of isolation, communication, and direct participation that were mentioned above. They respond by entering the categorical statuses and specialized social roles that characterize mass living in the new and emergent South. Thus the new Negro is recognized as a consumer market, a part of fandom, and a significant sector of television and radio audiences. Writing in this vein, Lewis and Hill observe, in part:

[2] Hylan Lewis and Mozell Hill, "Desegregation, Integration, and the Negro Community," *Annals* of the American Academy of Political and Social Science, Vol. 304 (March 1956), p. 122.
[3] Ibid., p. 122.

A significant clue to change is the fact that the most active organized and systematic current interest in the character, tastes, motivations, and expectations of the Negro is that of the market researchers. In their efforts to exploit consumer demand in the Negro community, they are actually creating a "Negro market" or reenforcing the myth. The Negro market does not represent a demand for special goods or services but rather an underrated demand for conventional and quality goods and services.[4]

But caste proscriptions still prevent Negroes from participating in some of the status-role configurations of the new Southern mass society. One accommodation to this situation is the creation and performance of a series of mass racial participation roles. Among the more familiar types are Negro block voters, secular associational members, and direct-action movement participants. Within this perspective it becomes possible to assess the meaning and portent of such phenomena as widespread political action; the large and growing membership of the NAACP; and the "spontaneous," grass-roots boycotts in Montgomery, Alabama; and Orangeburg, South Carolina. Other things being equal and change continuing in the present trend, we may expect such phenomena to increase in number and magnitude, thereby drawing greater numbers of Negroes directly and effectively into the economic, political, and social life of the Southern region.

[4] Ibid., p. 117

The Sit-Ins and the New Negro Student

CHARLES U. SMITH

During the late 1950's and the beginning of the 1960's college students throughout the United States began to take an active interest in the affairs of the nation and the world. This was in marked contrast to their behavior in the preceding decade when they were more quiescent and nonchalant. That Negro college students became more active in community and national affairs in this same period has been viewed with alarm and surprise by much of the white South. These Southerners regard this activity on the part of Negro students as an unexpected break with traditional patterns of "good racial relations."

It is eminently clear that the Negro college student has made a clean break with his erstwhile isolated and disassociated role in the community. This is especially true with regard to civil rights militancy. The sit-in demonstrations which have been carried on largely by Negro college students seem to have resulted from a variety of circumstances which have contributed to their changed self-image. Such circumstances include international developments, court decisions, fortuitous events and the general process of social change. These factors produced an awareness of and dissatisfaction with their previous role and status, and a revision of self-estimates by Negro college students.

Within the context of a local community and a single Negro college student body this paper seeks to examine and interpret the events and the process through which this new self-image developed. Specifically, this is an evaluation of occurrences among the Florida Agricultural and Mechanical University student body which may be somewhat illustrative of developments elsewhere.

Generally, the Negro college student had historically led a relatively sheltered life on the fringes of the white community. This sheltered existence had been tacitly forced upon the Negro college student because of segregation and partly because of the historical necessity for preserving racial "peace" and "good racial relations" by Negro college administrators seeking increased budgets, endowments and appropriations from wealthy white private benefactors and white state legislators. As a result of this situation the Negro college became a world unto itself with its own movie theater, recreational world, eating places, educational philosophy, and accommodating paternalism. In such a setting the Negro college student received little encouragement to enter into the affairs of the larger community as a private citizen, college student, and certainly as a militant exponent of civil rights.

It is reasonably safe to say that this isolated and patronizing world of the Negro college student received its greatest initial impetus from Booker T. Washington's famous Atlanta Exposition speech of 1895 and existed without serious challenge until World War II. One can hardly blame Washington for such a philosophy since it is quite likely that his time dictated such a procedure, if Negro college education was to survive at all. And it is certainly true that college educators since Washington found it the better expedient to continue along this line while hoping to advance the level of the Negro college as an institution of higher learning. Whatever the reasons for the establishment of the tradition of "sheltering" and isolation of the Negro college; and regardless of how justifiable such a practice may have been in the past, it is eminently clear that the Negro college student of today feels that this is a tradition that is not worthy of continuance and is obviously willing to work actively for its termination.

Bus Boycott

The first concrete indication of change in "conception of self" on the part of the Florida A and M University student body came not immediately after the Supreme Court decision of 1954, but two years later in 1956, when two hot and tired coeds sat next to a white woman on a crowded city bus. From this unplanned and fortuitous event arose the Tallahassee Bus Protest which had vast implications in changing the role of the Florida A and M University student body.

Through mass meetings and other demonstrations the FAMU student body was able to influence the majority of the Negro community of Tallahassee to boycott the city bus service for several months. They found that the adult members of the Negro community would listen to their ideas and cooperate with their efforts. They discovered that the state, local, and national press and other communications media were interested in what was going on in Tallahassee. They soon learned that although the white community disapproved of their actions and were angered and irritated by the protest and boycott, little, if any direct action of a punitive nature could be taken against them. They found also that college students enjoyed a kind of freedom from reprisal and a tolerance that was not shared by the non-student, adult citizens of the community. Thus began the emergence of the "new conception."

During and after the Bus Protest the FAMU students began to take more active roles in the affairs of the Tallahassee community and the State of Florida. The campus chapter of the NAACP became more active, and students began to work actively in efforts to get more Negroes registered to vote. More students began to attend the churches in the community and to attend off-campus lectures, forums, and discussion groups. In general, it appeared that there was greater concern about non-campus activities and problems on the part of the student body than there had ever been before.

A *"Cause Celebre"*

Three years later, in the Spring of 1959, another event, fortuitous in nature, served to bolster even more the changed conception of the students' role and status. On May 1, 1959 a FAMU coed was taken at gun point from her escort after a dance, by four white youths, each of whom proceeded to rape her. These four youths were apprehended the same night and confessions were obtained in less than six hours. Immediately upon learning of the situation the FAMU students held a mass meeting and vowed to see that justice was done. They discontinued attending classes for one day and used the time in speechmaking and singing, and rallying more and more of the students, as well as townspeople, to support them in their demands for speedy and total justice for the crime. National wire services, representatives of television networks, local, state, and national and international newsmen quickly gathered on the scene. The student leaders communicated by telephone, telegraph and cablegram with such faraway places as San Francisco, California; New York; Paris, France.

Because of their activity the rape of a Negro girl, historically commonplace in the South, became a local, state, national, international *cause celebre*. Subsequently, at the trial, news representatives were on hand to provide coverage from places as far away as New York and London. In a sense, the thorough prosecution and ultimate conviction of the four youths with life sentences was anticlimactic for a group of students who were now firmly convinced that their actions could influence public opinion and behavior on a local, state, national and international level.

With the prosecution of the rape case it appears that the break with the historical tradition of isolation from affairs of the larger community was complete. No longer was the FAMU student body a group of academic nonentities patiently and lackadaisically going about the business of reading, writing, and figuring. Now they were a group with status, prestige, fame, and a reputation for social and civic action to maintain. These students had found a place in the sun that was on a par with the performance of the numerous championship athletic teams and excellent musicians for which Florida A and M University had long been noted. To the proud traditions of athletic prowess and musical virtuosity was now added another—racial militancy.

Thus, by the time the sit-in demonstrations began in Greensboro in 1959 the FAMU student body were emotionally and spiritually prepared to enter into any legitimate fray on behalf of the rights of Negroes.

In the interest of accuracy it must be pointed out that not all of the FAMU student body participated in or actively supported the Bus Protest, the rape demonstrations or the sit-ins. A sizable portion of the group went about the normal and routine business of campus and college life during these incidents. There is no doubt, however, that a majority of the student body supported these activities morally, financially, or by direct participation.

Other Influences

While the activities described above seemed to have contributed to the preparedness and willingness of the FAMU students to engage in civil rights movements, at least four other factors are presently contributing to this "readiness" and "preparedness" and in the present view, will operate to maintain this psychological state for some time in the future.

First, there is the fact that Dr. Martin Luther King and his organization devoted to leadership in non-violent resistance (The Southern Christian Leadership Conference) has enormous influence on Negro youth.

Dr. King is particularly well-suited to appeal to the present-day Negro college student. He is highly trained academically; beyond reproach morally; superb oratorically; youthful, determined, and equally at home with the educated and non-educated.

The passive resistance technique provides a kind of outlet for college students to the civil rights arena which is especially appealing, in the absence of the ballot and financial resources.

Second, the activities of students abroad and the general struggles of non-white peoples in Africa and Asia, though not so significant in the early phases of activity by the FAMU students, will undoubtedly operate to maintain their interest in minority disprivileges.

Third, the sit-in demonstrations have attracted the attention and sympathy of white students, both north and south and will certainly cause the FAMU students as well as Negro college protesters everywhere to feel that their cause is just and that they will continue to get moral and financial support from these sympathetic groups.

Fourth, the belief in the justness of their cause has been and will be reinforced by the public pronouncement of Florida's Ex-Governor Leroy Collins that while he deplored the demonstrations he felt that the students were morally right in their demand for lunch counter service.

Fifth, while somewhat difficult to isolate objectively, this observer feels that an element of competition between Negro colleges has become a part of the civil rights struggle as participated in by Negro collegians.

As the expression "nigger-lover" is an effective deterrent to sympathetic identification with the problems of Negroes among whites, so the expression "handkerchief-head" is used among present-day Negro students to refer to those who are afraid and unwilling to join the battle for greater civil rights; and is an epithet so powerful that students will go to almost any lengths to avoid its application to them individually or collectively.

Uninformed persons have raised the cry that "outside agitators" have sparked the sit-in demonstrations in Tallahassee. The facts simply do not validate this claim. Over ninety-five per cent of the entire student body at FAMU is from Florida, including the student body president and the great majority of the members of the Student Government Association. All six of the students convicted and who served the jail sentences were native Floridians. Adult, non-student participation in Tallahassee has been largely confined to arranging bail bonds and assisting with the procurement of legal counsel for the students.

However difficult the realization may be, the hard fact is that from the student body at FAMU are slowly but surely emerging representatives of a "new Negro," with attitudes and behaviors completely alien to tradition; a "new Negro" who is able to develop his own leadership and conviction. This "new Negro" is baffling and irritating to much of the white community; and the lengths to which he is prepared to go—though they may be admired and respected—are not fully understood by members of the Negro community who have lived so long with *Plessy* vs *Ferguson.*

SECTION TWO

SECTION TWO

Foreword: Beginning the Future:
Equal Achievement and Integration

EARL RAAB

The gap between equal opportunity and equal achievement has been most striking in the cities of the North and West, which have outlawed and begun to modify practices of racial discrimination. Particularly striking in these cities is the gap between desegregation and integration, most clearly revealed in the public schools.

Over 90 per cent of the students are Negro or Puerto Rican in about 13 per cent of the elementary schools in New York City. About 99 per cent of the students are Negro in 14 per cent of Philadelphia's public schools. At least 85 per cent of the students are Negro or Mexican-American in almost 20 per cent of the elementary schools in Los Angeles. Almost half of the Negro elementary school children in Detroit attend schools which are more than 80 per cent Negro.

In all of these cities, deliberate segregation is strictly prohibited. Even the back-door practice of gerrymandering school districts is becoming a thing of the past. Yet, in these and many other northern and western cities, the problem of concentrated white or non-white schools has become steadily worse rather than better.

The reasons are not mysterious. School populations are determined by residential patterns. The proportions of Negroes in these cities have risen rapidly, and the Negro ghettos have become correspondingly more dense.

Housing discrimination is only one factor in the build-up of these racial ghettos. In most of the northern and western cities there were fewer all-white neighborhoods in 1960 than in 1950, there were fewer "restricted" areas, but there were still more and larger ghettos. In San Francisco, there were 3 census tracts in 1950 which were over 75 per cent non-white; in 1960, there were 7 such census tracts. Discrimination was not disappearing as fast as Negro populations were gathering. But the over-riding factor was the ghettoized economic status of the Negro community; housing patterns reflect economic patterns. And school patterns reflect housing patterns.

To complete the vicious circle, achievement levels are finally grounded in these climactic school patterns. The New York City schools found that the reading levels of eighth-grade pupils in predominantly non-white schools were on the average almost two and a half years behind the pupils in predominantly white schools. Throughout the country, academic achievement is lower in predominantly Negro schools, even though the capacity for achievement is just as high as in other schools. School and neighborhood ghettos are, among other things, cultural and aspirational ghettos.

Among the symptomatic effects is a higher rate of "dropout" from predominantly Negro high schools. It has been estimated that about a third of America's high school students drop out before they are graduated. A disproportionate number of these are Negro students. In one study of four Connecticut high school districts, there were about 60 per cent more drop-outs among Negroes than among whites.

In an age of automation, such "school-leavers" are increasingly at an economic disadvantage. In the last several years, the number of service workers in the country for the first time exceeded the number of production workers.

There seems to be a higher rate of "normal" unemployment, and certainly a diminishing opportunity for unskilled labor. In the Connecticut study, about one-fourth of the male students who had dropped out of high school the year before were unemployed. About twice as many Negro as white boys had never held any job since leaving school.

The drop-out situation also contrasts sharply with rising college populations. While a third of those students who enter high school drop out before graduation, more than half of those who graduate are now going on to college. This widening cleavage in our society is partly an urban-suburban cleavage and a racial cleavage.

This vicious circle of low economic status, ghetto-ized housing, segregated schooling, sub-standard school achievement, leading back to low economic status, tends to retard integration and equal achievement, even where discrimination and formal segregation are on the decrease.

There has consequently developed a belief that integration must be advanced more quickly and directly than is apparently possible through the neutralism of civil rights, i.e., the enforced race blindness of government, schools, employers, labor unions and housing purveyors. Perhaps the doctrine of race blindness must be supplemented by a policy of constructive "race consciousness" in order actively to promote integration and equal achievement. But how?

Complicating the problem of integration in one historical sense, while relieving it in another, is the fact that these are not captive or subjugated pools of Negro population as they were in the old South. As separate communities they are exercising increasing political weight. There are internal political and economic impulses towards building rather than breaking down separate community organization. These impulses match a mood of "Negro nationalism" emergent among some sections of the Negro population.

There are, of course, other groups in American life subject to discrimination and segregation, including a quarter of a million Chinese-Americans, a half million Japanese-Americans, perhaps a million Puerto Ricans and 4 million Mexican-Americans.

There are also 5 million Jews in America who have been subject to deep-running currents of bigotry in the last half-century, but the direction, and often the nature, of this problem is quite different from that of racial bigotry. Skin color is not a factor. The major veins of anti-Semitism in this country have been a kind of home-grown social snobbery on one hand, and, on the other, a specific racist mystique inherited from Europe, the ideology of anti-Semitism. The potential for violent outbreak of anti-Semitic racism cannot be accurately measured by the extent of or the lack of discrimination, or even by attitude polls. This was one indelible lesson taught by German history between World Wars I and II. But the demonstrable reduction of discrimination against American Jews in the past two decades has had its own significance. Residential ghettos have, in the main, disappeared. Indeed, Jews are joining in the white-skinned, middle-class movement to the suburbs. Integration on almost every level of community life becomes ever more thoroughgoing. There are growing problems of interreligious relations, outside the framework of bigotry; there are new problems of group identity, as external restraints lift; for modern generations there will always be an active concern with the possible recrudescence of political anti-Semitism. But less and less is the problem for American Jews one of segregation or unequal opportunity, of integration or equal group achievement.

Nor are Chinese-American and Japanese-American populations significantly involved in the growing complex of problems treated here. Because of size, history, and degree of self-employment, both groups have achieved a relatively high educational and economic level. Japanese-Americans are spread widely through both rural and urban areas, mainly in the West, and nowhere present the threat of an insoluble population lump. More than half of the Chinese-American population is in the San Francisco area where some ghetto-like conditions do prevail. However, this ghetto presents no different social problem than it did a generation ago, and is largely supported by unique internal conditions.

On the other hand, both the Puerto Rican and Mexican-American populations share the low achievement levels of the Negro population in several metropolitan centers. At least 80 per cent of the Puerto Rican population on the mainland is in New York City. It is estimated that close to half a million people of Mexican descent are in Los Angeles, matching the Negro population in that city. There are other concentrations of Mexican-American population in Southwestern cities, although there is also much movement of this group between the fields and the cities. The problems of integration and achievement for these groups are aggravated by language barriers which do not exist for the Negro, although the color line is sometimes less severe. But, with these regional modifications, the newer aspects of the race-relations problems revolve around 19 million Negroes, and the possible development of self-perpetuating Negro ghettos in the metropolitan centers of the North and West.

In "The Metropolitan Area as a Racial Problem," Morton Grodzins provides a classic description of the emerging Northern metropolis, and a survey of some of the possibilities for remedy.

In "Can Intergroup Quotas Be Benign?" Dan Dodson deals specifically with some of the proposals for constructive "race consciousness."

In "Is 'Integration' Possible in New York Schools?" Nathan Glazer describes the frustrations encountered by one metropolis, tangled in the "disasters of history," in its attempts to advance integration through the schools.

In "Schools and Northern Negro Slums," James B. Conant concentrates on the problems of achievement in predominantly non-white slum schools. He suggests that ultimate social integration and social cohesion may depend more on equalizing achievement levels than on physical integration in the schools, and that the former is a more realistic goal than the latter.

Some special problems of integration are described by Leonard Broom and Eshref Shevky in "Mexicans in the United States," and by Joseph P. Fitzpatrick in "The Adjustment of Puerto Ricans to New York City."

In "The Black Muslims of America," C. Eric Lincoln analyzes the extreme wing of the Negro nationalist sentiment.

The Metropolitan Area as a
Racial Problem

MORTON GRODZINS

Almost nothing is being done today to meet what is likely to be the nation's most pressing social problem tomorrow. The problem can be simply stated in all its bleakness: many central cities of the great metropolitan areas of the United States are fast becoming lower class, largely Negro slums.

I. THE GREAT SCHISM OF POPULATION

Some 113 million people, more than half the population of the United States, now live in what the Bureau of the Census defines as a standard metropolitan area: a central city of at least 50 thousand population with its ring of satellite communities "essentially metropolitan in character and socially and economically integrated with the central city." Fewer than one-third of the nation's population lived within these areas in 1900; and it is estimated that 70 per cent of the nation's total population will be metropolitan area dwellers by 1975.

The fifteen largest metropolitan areas contain almost half of the total metropolitan population and almost one-third of the nation's.[1] These areas attract the largest num-

---

[1] These are the fifteen metropolitan areas which had populations over one million in 1950 and over one million and a quarter in 1960: New York—northeastern New Jersey, Los An-

ber of Negro in-migrants from the South, and in them, generally, Negroes constitute a larger proportion of the total population. The consequences of the urban-suburban racial and class bifurcation, therefore, are most acute in these largest metropolitan areas. Some smaller metropolitan areas face the same problems in less acute form while others, because of their small number of Negroes, do not face them at all.

For several decades the Negro population of the great cities has been increasing more rapidly than the white population. The great changes come in time of full employment, and an explosive growth, as measured by the decennial censuses, took place between 1940 and 1950. In that decade, the total population of the fifteen largest metropolitan areas increased by 19 per cent, the total Negro percentage gain (65.1 per cent) being more than four times greater than the white increase (15.6 per cent). Negroes increased proportionately more rapidly in both central cities and suburbs, but the significant growth differential was inside the great cities. Whites increased by 3.7 per cent, Negroes 67.8 per cent. The Negro population at least doubled in four central cities while whites in five cities decreased in number.

As late as 1950 non-whites constituted only a minor fraction of the total population in most of the central cities of the fourteen largest metropolitan areas. Washington, D. C., with non-whites totalling 35.4 per cent of total population, and Baltimore (23.8 per cent) had the largest group of non-whites in proportion to total population. In addition to these, only three other cities had 1950 Negro populations in excess of 15 per cent; three had less than 10 per cent.

---

geles, Chicago, Philadelphia, Detroit, San Francisco, Boston, Pittsburgh, St. Louis, Washington, Cleveland, Baltimore, Newark, Minneapolis, and Buffalo.

The Metropolitan Area as a Racial Problem

Continued Negro migration, the comparatively greater rate of natural increase among non-whites, and the exodus of whites to the suburbs continues to raise dramatically the proportion of non-whites in central cities. In 1960, eight of these fifteen cities had Negro populations in excess of 15 per cent, as against five of the cities in 1950. Indeed, 1960 Negro populations in six of the cities—Baltimore, Cleveland, Detroit, Philadelphia, St. Louis, Washington—exceeded 25 per cent.

Chicago is expected to be one-third Negro by 1970.

New York City officials have forecast that in 1970 Negroes and Puerto Ricans together will constitute 45 per cent of the population of Manhattan and nearly one-third of the entire city. Washington, D. C. already has an actual Negro majority.

Estimates of future population trends must take into account some reurbanization of white suburbanites as the proportion of older people increases and the suburbs become less attractive to those whose children have grown up and left home. Even making allowances for shifts of this sort, all evidence makes it highly probable that within 30 years Negroes will constitute from 25 to 50 per cent of the total population in at least 10 of the 14 largest central cities.

The suburbs of the metropolitan areas exhibit very different population trends. Negroes made up only 4 per cent of their population in 1940 and less than 5 per cent in 1950. (Central city non-whites were 9 per cent of total population in 1940, 13.2 per cent in 1950.)

Some suburban areas experienced non-white percentage gains and even the fourteen-area totals show Negro increases greater than white ones. But the actual number of Negroes was small. A suburban non-white gain of 130 per cent in Minneapolis-St. Paul, for example, represented an actual increase of exactly 337 persons. Moreover, even the non-white "suburban" increases noted are rarely to the suburbs themselves. Rather they largely represent Negro migration to the smaller industrial towns within the metropolitan rings of the central cities. Special censuses made of suburban places since 1950 strengthen the impression of Negro exclusion. There is evidence of absolute decreases in the numbers of Negroes in some suburban areas; in other areas there has been a movement of one or two non-white families into all-white communities. The only statistically significant suburban growth of Negro population, however, has taken place in industrial fringe cities—Gary, Indiana, for example—or in segregated Negro dormitory communities—Robbins, Illinois, for example.

There is no exception in the 14 cities to the pattern of a widening gap between Negro city percentages and Negro suburban percentages. Where Negroes in 1940 were proportionally most numerous in both central cities and suburbs (as in Baltimore and Washington, D. C.), the subsequent decade saw non-whites decrease markedly as a percentage of suburban populations and increase markedly as a percentage of central city populations. This record very likely traces the future for other cities whose urban-suburban population distribution by race in 1960 approximated the 1940 distribution of Baltimore and Washington.

The general picture of the future is clear enough: large non-white concentrates (in a few cases, majorities) in the principal central cities; large white majorities, with segregated Negro enclaves, in the areas outside.

II. Growth Patterns Within Cities

The pattern of Negro population growth within the central cities follows established and well-understood patterns. It is based upon in-migration from the South, and it is accelerated by a larger rate of natural increase of the non-white in-migrants in comparison with the older white residents. Migration has been the source of the largest increase in most non-southern cities, and continued industrial expansion may actually increase this movement in the years immediately ahead. The "push" from the South may grow stronger as the consequence of growing white antagonisms following attempts to enforce the Supreme Court's non-segregation decisions. And the "pull" of the northern cities may become more forceful as the Negro communities there become larger and more firmly established and as information concerning job and other opportunities correspondingly flows back to relatives and friends. On the other hand, the relatively more rapid natural increase of Negroes, in comparison with white residents, might be expected to become less striking with the passage of years as the immigrant Negro population comes closer to the smaller-family characteristics of the urban dweller.

The spatial expansion of Negro population in the larger cities follows roughly similar patterns. One universal rule is that residential concentrations are segregated. In every major city with a considerable number of Negroes there exists a "black belt" or a series of "black areas." In Chicago, 79 per cent of all Negroes in 1950 lived in census tracts in which at least 75 per cent of the residents were Negroes. At the opposite extreme, 84 per cent of the non-Negroes resided in census tracts in which less than 1 per cent of the residents were Negroes and the disparity would be even higher if Negro servants "living in" were not counted. Chicago's segregation pattern is somewhat extreme, but all cities follow this pattern. Negroes live preponderantly or exclusively with Negroes, whites with whites.

A second rule is equally general: once an urban area begins to swing from predominant white to predominant Negro occupancy, the change is rarely reversed. Between 1920 and 1950 in Chicago there are no cases in which areas of predominantly Negro residents reverted to areas of white occupancy. More than this, a neighborhood with a substantial proportion of Negroes (say 25 per cent) rarely retains its mixed character for a considerable period of time. The Duncans, in their intensive study of neighborhood changes in Chicago,[2] found not a single instance between 1940 and 1950 of a census tract "with mixed population (25–75 per cent non-white) in which succession from white to Negro occupancy was arrested" though, as they remark, the succession was more rapid in some tracts than in others. Postwar programs of public housing and urban renewal have somewhat altered this rule, in some cases establishing new Negro concentrates where they had not previously existed and in others demonstrating that relatively stable interracial patterns of living can be achieved. But new housing programs in predominantly Negro areas have for the most part meant the simple exchange of one Negro population group for another; and urban renewal programs, by displacing Negro families in one area, have frequently had the effect of hastening the succession of adjacent areas to all-Negro occupancy.

A third generalization is that the pattern of Negro residential expansion is from the core of the city outward. The original concentration is almost everywhere near the center of the city. It subsequently expands radially or in concentric circles. A map by zones for virtually every city with a sizeable Negro population shows higher percentages of Negro residence in areas closest to the city center with decreasing proportions as the distance from the city center increases.

A fourth generalization is also possible. The Negro population moves generally into areas already characterized by high residential mobility. Furthermore, there is a rough

[2] Otis D. Duncan and Beverly Duncan, *The Negro Population of Chicago,* (Chicago: University of Chicago Press, 1957) p. 120

comparability between the social characteristics of the in-migrant Negro population and the out-migrant white population with respect to such factors as educational attainment, rate of unemployment, room crowding, home ownership, and white collar employment. Lower-class Negroes, in other words, tend to move into lower-class neighborhoods; middle-class Negroes into middle-class neighborhoods. The "piling up" process—the gross overcrowding of dwellings and areas—occurs only after the transition from white to Negro dominance has taken place.

III. THE "TIPPING" MECHANISM

The process by which whites of the central cities leave areas of Negro in-migration can be understood as one in the social-psychology of "tipping a neighborhood." The variations are numerous, but the theme is universal. Some white residents will not accept Negroes as neighbors under any conditions. But others, sometimes willingly as a badge of liberality, sometimes with trepidation, will not move if a relatively small number of Negroes move into the same neighborhood, the same block, or the same apartment building. Once the proportion of non-whites exceeds the limits of the neighborhood's tolerance for interracial living (this is the "tip point"), the whites move out. The proportion of Negroes who will be accepted before the tip point is reached varies from city to city and from neighborhood to neighborhood.

The process is not the simple one of "flight" that is a part of the real estate mythology of changing neighborhoods. It may take a number of years before the "invaded" neighborhood becomes an all-Negro one. Nor is the phenomenon uniformly one in which Negroes "push" whites out. As already noted, areas of heavy Negro in-migration are most often areas already characterized by high mobility; and the process of Negroes taking up vacancies as they occur cannot be conceived as one in which the old residents have been "pushed." This is to say that tipping may come slowly and does not necessarily indicate any immediate downgrading of the given neighborhood. What it signifies is the unwillingness of white groups to live in proximity to large numbers of Negroes.

Many people in many ways for many purposes have explored how the tip point operates. Real estate operators, seeking the higher revenues that come with Negro overcrowding, talk freely among themselves about "tipping a building" or "tipping a neighborhood." (Sometimes this can be done by selling a single house to a "block busting" family.) Quakers in the Philadelphia suburbs of Concord Park and Greenbelt Knoll have utilized the tip point for the opposite purpose: to build interracial communities. They have concluded that this goal can be achieved only if the proportion of Negroes is rigidly controlled and does not exceed the point at which whites (even Quakers) will refuse to participate. An official of these developments has written: "Early in our sales program we found that white buyers would not buy without assurance that Negroes would be in a minority."

Public housing officials have faced the tip-point phenomenon from another angle. In some Eastern cities it is possible to maintain low cost housing projects on an interracial basis as long as non-whites do not exceed roughly 20 per cent of the total residents. Once this point is reached, whites will not remain in, or move into, the project. One method used to combat the process of tipping public housing has been to raise rents. This has the effect of decreasing the number of Negroes who can afford to live in the projects. So the tip point leads to a shifting of public housing goals, subordinating the first principle of low rentals to that of maintaining interracial occupancy.

In a few areas around the country Negroes and whites live side by side without fuss or fanfare. This is true even in Chicago, where segregation patterns are extreme, and examples of "open occupancy" can be found from New York to San Francisco. Furthermore, in recent years, there has been a tendency for a single Negro family—usually of considerable income and of the professions—to find a dwelling in an all-white neighborhood. In every such case of "interracial living," however, some factor—economic or other—limits the ingress of Negro residents.

Education and community organization can extend tolerance and thus increase the proportion of Negroes in a given area before the tip point is reached. But the limits have not proved to be infinitely elastic. Even where goodwill, community effort, and financing have been maximized, the psychology of tipping has operated. The only interracial communities in the United States, with the exception of some abject slums, are those where limits exist upon the influx of non-whites.

IV. Patterns of Suburban Exclusion

The sheer cost of suburban housing excludes Negroes from many suburban areas. Furthermore, the social satisfactions of slum or near-slum existence for a homogeneous population have been insufficiently studied, and it is undoubtedly true that many Negro urban dwellers would not easily exchange life in all-Negro big-city neighborhoods for interracial suburban homes, even if moderately priced. The crucial fact, however, is that Negroes do not have any free choice in the matter. They are excluded from suburbia by a wide variety of devices.

Social antagonisms of suburban communities are themselves effective. Where it is plainly understood that Negroes are not wanted, Negro suburbanization is for all practical purposes impossible. In addition, suburban communities use their control of zoning, subdivision, and building regulations to achieve exclusion. Minimum lot sizes are increased to two or more acres; requirements for expensive street improvements are made—and then waived only in favor of "desirable" developments; large-scale building operations are defined as "business" for zoning purposes, thus excluding the possibility of low or moderate income suburban building; the suburb itself purchases all vacant land parcels that are large enough for subdivision and resells only to favored purchasers; builders are required to obtain certificates from the school board that educational accommodation will be adequate for the new residences; ordinances regulating "look alike" features or requiring certain building materials make home building expensive.

Where legal barriers of this sort are not sufficient to maintain a "white only" policy, land use controls are used informally—and of course illegally—to exclude Negroes. A Philadelphia builder recently told an interviewer that he would very much like to sell suburban houses to Negroes, but that it was impossible because it would ruin him economically. "If I sold just one suburban home to a Negro, the local building inspectors would have me moving pipes three-eighths of an inch every afternoon in every one of the places I was building; and moving a pipe three-eighths of an inch is mighty expensive if you have to do it in concrete."

These practices are combined with social and economic pressures upon white owners of older homes and upon real estate brokers. Mortgage bankers habitually discriminate against the Negro buyer in the white neighborhood, and not always for purely economic reasons. Where all else fails, suburban residents have often turned to violence to prevent Negro occupancy. The total suburban facade is relatively impenetrable.

Suburban restrictions are everywhere aimed at Negroes as a racial group and not simply against people of low or moderate income. When such restrictions are applied uniformly, they of course also affect whites. But even this has an indirect effect upon the Negro concentrates within the cities. If middle- and lower-class whites who live next door to the slums were able to move to the suburbs, their places would quickly be taken by the slum-dwellers, especially those Negroes whose presence in the slums is due less to income than to the prejudice which excludes them from more desirable places. By raising the price of housing in the suburbs, land use regulations reduce the movement of the white middle and lower classes out of the city. And this in turn holds the slum-dweller in the slums and, accordingly, the Negro in the ghetto.

V. Consequences of Population Distribution

Some of the consequences of the urban-suburban racial and class schism are already apparent, and others can be reasonably predicted.

Social Consequences

Within the cities the first result is a spreading of slums. There is no free market for Negro housing. The Negro population always increases faster than the living space available to it. New areas that open up to Negro residence become grossly overcrowded by conversion of one-family houses to multiple dwellings and by squeezing two or more Negro families into apartments previously occupied by a single white one. Though complete statistical evidence is lacking, it is likely that Negroes pay substantially more rent for such accommodations than do whites, and the higher rent itself produces higher densities. Housing occupied by Negroes is more crowded, more dilapidated, and more lacking in amenities such as private baths than housing occupied by whites with equivalent incomes.

Income factors account in part for the condition of life of the Negro community. Negroes are heavily over-represented in low income jobs: in the menial services, in unskilled and semi-skilled factory labor, and in "dirty work" generally. In this respect they are not unlike some earlier immigrants to the city; the Irish and the Poles, for example, also settled mainly in the slums.

Like previous newcomers to the city tasting the freedom of urban life for the first time, a significant portion of the Negro group does not possess the stable patterns of thought and action that characterize the "better" older inhabitants. And, as with all immigrant groups, old community patterns of control do not operate well in the new environment. Family disorganization among urban Negroes is high as measured by such indices as broken marriages, families headed by females, and unrelated individuals living in the same household. The development of social stabilization pivoted on family and community ties takes place against great odds. How does a mother keep her teen-age son off the streets if an entire family must eat, sleep, and live in a single room? What utility can be found in sobriety among a society of drinkers and in a block of taverns? What opportunity for quiet amidst the din of a tightly packed, restless neighborhood?

The conditions of urban life, rather than socializing new Negro residents to "desirable" life patterns, frequently have the opposite effect. They encourage rowdiness, casual and competitive sexuality, and a readiness for combat. The result is that the neighborhoods acquired by Negro residents eventually spiral downward. Disease and crime rates are high. Family stability is further prejudiced. Filth accumulates. The slum spreads outward.

These very conditions of life in the predominantly Negro neighborhoods lead the larger population to resist the expansion of Negro residential areas. The racial attribute—skin color—is added to the social attributes of lower class behavior. And while Negroes, like other urban immigrants, can readily lose undesirable social attributes, they cannot lose their color. They therefore do not have the mobility of other immigrant groups. They are racially blocked, whatever their social *bona fides*.

The Negro "black belts" of the great American cities as a consequence are by no means homogeneous. The very concentration of population within them plus the visible badge of color give them a spurious air of likeness. They contain, in fact, wide ranges of every social attribute: from illiteracy to high learning, from filth to hospital-like hygienic standards, from poverty to riches, from political backwardness to sophistication. Though the casual observer of the "black belt" neighborhoods sees only slums, the fact is that in every such area there are sub-areas, frequently on the periphery of the high-density mass, that are anything but slums. These are usually neighborhoods of newest acquisition, inhabited by the well-to-do of the Negro community. Density is low, lawns and gardens are well-tended, church attendance is high, neatness and cleanliness are apparent, parental standards of propriety for children higher than for comparable white groups.

Negro neighborhoods in the shadows of white luxury apartments are not unknown; but the more usual pattern is for low-income non-Negroes to occupy a buffer zone between all-Negro and the better white neighborhoods. Some of these are themselves new migrants to the city: rural white Southerners and Japanese-Americans in Chicago, Puerto Ricans in New York, for example. Others are old residents on the lower ends of the income scale, people who, like the Negroes themselves, do not find success in life, or life itself, easy.

With the exodus of middle and upper classes to the suburbs, lower-income groups constitute a larger and larger fraction of the population of the central cities. Members of these groups generally exhibit a greater degree of intolerance and racial prejudice than do other whites. And the increasing juxtaposing of the Negro and the low-income non-Negro populations produces increased interracial tensions. Shirley Star of the National Opinion Research Center has shown that the greatest white animosity towards Negroes is found on the edge of the expanding Negro residential areas where whites fear their block or neighborhood will soon be "invaded." In these lower class and lower-middle class transitional areas, violence is incipient. Individual differences within the minority group are ignored. A young white resident of such an area in Chicago recently beat a Negro to death with a hammer. "I just wanted to get one of them," he explained, "which one didn't matter."

The total situation produces Negro communities in which people live their whole lives without, or with minimum, contact with the other race. With a Negro population numbering in the hundreds of thousands, and with this population densely concentrated, one can live, eat, shop, work, play, and die in a completely Negro community. The social isolation of the northern urban Negro is, for very large numbers, more complete than it ever was for the Negro rural resident in the South.

Even in education, the urban residential segregation of the non-southern cities has produced consequences that are not dissimilar to what the South is trying to maintain by the use of violence and unconstitutional law. If segregation is defined not in legal terms but in the numbers of students who attend all-Negro schools, then it is undoubtedly true that more Negro students are segregated in the schools of New York and Chicago than in any other cities or some states.

This general picture of segregation needs some qualification. A small number of church groups have succeeded in building interracial congregations. Qualified Negro workers are finding employment in places previously barred to them, not only in manufacturing, but also in the professions and in retail establishments. On a few blocks in urban America, Negroes and whites have demonstrated that they can live together as neighbors. Labor unions, though traditionally anti-Negro, have in some places accepted Negroes as full partners in leadership as well as membership.

These are evidences of advances toward social integration. Other advances have been made within the Negro community itself. As this community in a given city grows larger, satisfactory career lines, economic security, and the home and community life that accompany such developments become possible. Here, however, Negroes and whites meet each other across separate societies rather than within a single group. The Negro shares with whites the better things of life, but he does so in isolation with other Negroes. The disadvantaged segregated community even produces advantages for some individuals within it, providing protected markets for Negro professionals and businessmen and protected constituencies for Negro political and church leaders. Yet even those who profit from segregation suffer from it. They feel the pin-pricks as well as the sledges of discrimination, and they must suppress their dissatisfaction in accordance with standards of conduct expected of all "better" people, whatever their race.

The larger evidence is neither that of social integration nor of intra-community social gains. Rather it is evidence pointing to the expansion of Negro slums within the largest

cities and the separation of whites and Negroes by intra-
city neighborhoods and especially on central city-suburban
lines.

Economic Consequences

Population shifts bring with them major economic consequences. Of first importance is the further decline of a
large segment of business activity and associated property
values, in the central cities. For reasons only remotely related—or unrelated—to the Negro-white population distribution, the economic feasibility of decentralized retail
shopping has already been demonstrated. Suburban shopping centers have captured a large segment of the market
in clothing, furniture, and other consumption goods; almost
everywhere the "downtown" shops of the central cities
have lost ground, absolutely and proportionally, to the
peripheral developments. Retail sales in the central business district of Chicago decreased by 5 per cent between
1948 and 1954, while sales in the metropolitan area outside the city increased by 53 per cent. The relative sales
loss of downtown areas has been even greater in other
central cities.

Further developments can be foreseen. The downtown
stores, with non-white and low-income customers more and
more predominant in their clientele, will tend to concen-
trate on cheaper merchandise. " 'Borax' for downtown,
Herman Miller for the suburb," is already a slogan of the
furniture business. The decline of the central-city department store will be accompanied by a general deterioration
of the downtown area. There are some striking exceptions,
most notably in mid-town Manhattan. But in most cities
—Chicago, Boston, Los Angeles are good examples—the
main streets are becoming infested with sucker joints for
tourists: all night jewelry auctions, bargain linens and

cheap neckties, hamburger stands and jazz dives. The slums, in other words, are spreading to the central business districts.

A further, though more problematic, development is that the offices of the larger corporations will join the flight from the city, taking along with them their servicing businesses: banks, law offices, advertising agencies, and others. The rapid development of closed circuit television, facsimile reproduction, and other technical aids relieves these businesses of the necessity of clustering at a central point. Their exodus from the city is already underway. New highways will make it easier in many places to get from one suburb to another than from suburb to downtown; and the losses of giving up central headquarters can be amortized over a number of years, frequently at considerable tax savings. Even the downtown hotel is likely to give way to the suburban motel except for convention purposes, an incidental further boost to the honkey-tonk development within the downtown business areas.

The rule seems to be a simple one: retail trade, the white collar shops, and the service industries will follow population. (Once their exodus is well underway, they also lead population.) The same general rule at least partially applies for manufacturing: the greatest suburbanization of manufacturing has taken place in those metropolitan areas where there has also been the most marked suburbanization of population, and some evidence indicates that manufacturing precedes population, rather than vice versa. Though the central cities have lost some manufacturing to both suburban and non-metropolitan areas, they have nevertheless maintained the preponderant share of the nation's total manufacturing enterprise. As Kitagawa and Bogue have shown, "the over-all spatial distribution [of manufacturing] in the United States has changed comparatively little in the past 50 years."[3] The relative immobility of heavy industry has the result of fixing the laboring and semi-skilled groups, including large numbers of Negroes, within the central cities.

Even a conservative view must anticipate the exodus of a large segment of retail and other non-manufacturing businesses from downtown centers. Abandonment of these centers will lead to a host of municipal problems, not least of which is the loss of a substantial tax base. These economic developments are at once a step towards, and a consequence of, the city-suburban bifurcation of races that promises to transform many central cities into lower class ethnic islands. Successful attempts by central cities to encourage the establishment of new manufacturing plants as a means of rebuilding their tax base will of course hasten this process.

Political Consequences

Whatever the melancholy resemblance between older segregation patterns of the rural South and newer ones of the urban North, one important fact is different: the Negroes of the North possess the suffrage. How will they use it if they become the majority group—or at least the largest single group—in some of the great cities of the nation?

The most likely political development is the organization of Negroes for ends conceived narrowly to the advantage of the Negro community. Such a political effort might aim to destroy zoning and building restrictions for the immediate purpose of enlarging opportunities for desperately

[3] Evelyn M. Kitagawa and Donald J. Bogue, *Suburbanization of Manufacturing Activity Within Standard Metropolitan Areas* (Published jointly by Scripps Foundation for Research in Population Problems, Miami University, and Population Research and Training Center, University of Chicago), 1955, p. 15

needed Negro housing against stubborn social pressures. If successful, the outcome might merely extend the Negro ghetto and cause a further departure of white populations to the suburbs. Yet the short-run political appeal of this action cannot be denied.

What the Negroes seek for themselves in Chicago in 1975 or 1985 might not be any more selfishly conceived than what Irish-dominated city councils in Boston and New York have sought in the past. In one essential field, Negro leadership may be more advantageous to the whole population: lacking devotion to the parochial schools, it would not be mean in the support of public schools. The rub lies in the very visibility of Negro domination. Even on the assumption of Negro leaders and followers demonstrating wisdom and forbearance, what would be the consequence in one or more major cities of the city councils becoming predominantly Negro? What will be the situation in a state legislature when the largest group of big-city representatives are Negroes?

At the very least, cities politically dominated by Negroes will find it more difficult to bring about the urban-suburban cooperation so badly needed in so many fields. They will find greatly exacerbated what is already keenly felt in a majority of states: the conflict between the great urban center and the rural "downstate" or "upstate" areas. Similar unfortunate effects will follow in the national Congress, once a number of large cities are largely represented by Negro congressmen. The pitting of whites against Negroes, and of white policies against Negro policies, does not await actual Negro urban domination. The cry has already been raised in state legislatures. The conflict can only grow more acute as race and class become increasingly coterminous with local government boundaries.

In the long run, it is highly unlikely that the white population will allow Negroes to become dominant in the cities without resistance. The cultural and economic stakes are too high. One countermeasure will surely present itself to the suburbanites: to annex the suburbs, with their predominantly white populations, to the cities. This will be a historic reversal of the traditional suburban antipathy to annexation. But in the perception of suburbanites it will be justified: they will be annexing the city to the suburbs.

The use of annexation to curb Negro political powers is already underway. It was an explicit argument used by political leaders favoring an annexation to Nashville in 1952. And other recent annexations, largely confined to the South, have taken place at least partially to deny Negroes political powers they would otherwise achieve.

Other actions to the same end can be expected, especially the gerrymandering of Negro populations so as to deny them equitable representation in legislative bodies of city, state, and nation. Tuskegee, Alabama, was gerrymandered in 1957 to exclude all but a handful of Negro voters from city elections, and steps are currently under way to divide Macon County among five neighboring counties. Negroes have long lived within the city, and the county has for many years been preponderantly Negro, but only recently have the Negroes exercised their franchise in any numbers. In the border city of Cincinnati, fear of growing Negro political power was an important reason for the 1957 action that repealed proportional representation and subsequently defeated the reform City Charter Committee. During the campaign over proportional representation, whispering campaigns urged defeat of the system in order to prevent Theodore M. Berry, Negro vice-mayor, from becoming mayor, as well as to prevent Negroes from moving into white neighborhoods. The total political picture of continued racial bifurcation forecasts a new round of political repression aimed at Negroes. For this one, they will be better armed—effective numbers, economic strength, political sophistication, and allies in the white population.

VI. Towards Solutions

If racial separation and segregation lead to evil consequences, the cure is obvious; the separation should be ended. For no problem is a solution more easily stated: white populations should be brought back into the central cities, and Negroes should be allowed to choose freely where they want to live in all areas of central cities and suburbs alike. No solution is more difficult to implement.

Racial exclusiveness may be conceived as an "American dilemma" in moral terms, or a Marxian problem of class antagonisms, or a Freudian expression of instinctual attractions and cultural taboos. From these perspectives the "race problem" may be solved, if at all, only through the slow marches of gradual social change. Neither laws, nor adult education, nor *ad hoc* institutional programs can be decisive.

It can certainly be assumed that for a long time for some people in some places no program of residential integration will be palatable or acceptable. Yet it is also true that people are not frozen in antagonistic attitudes, that change is possible, and that the change can best be achieved by actual successful experiences in interracial living. Most importantly, plans can be built upon the great diversity of outlook and attitude among the urban populations of mid-century America.

The most important general step to be taken is to remove the restrictions on where Negroes may live. This is, in the first place, an act of simple justice. Of greater relevance here, if non-whites possessed genuine residential mobility, it would go a long way toward eliminating the great social costs of the present population distribution. From free movement, it follows that (1) there would be less overcrowding in Negro areas; (2) there would be fewer and smaller all-Negro neighborhoods; and (3) individual Negroes would self-selectively distribute themselves, as white populations do, among neighborhoods whose social characteristics are roughly homogeneous and roughly similar to their own.

It should not be supposed that the removal of restrictions would end Negro residential concentrations. Income factors alone will confine many Negroes to the least desirable residential areas for a long time to come. Considerations of sociability are also an important concentrating factor. Investments in businesses and living quarters will keep even many of those who can afford to move as residents of all-Negro areas. Yet many Negroes now live in Negro neighborhoods simply because they have no other place to go. With the occupational upgrading and increased income that Negroes are achieving in ever-growing numbers, there is no doubt that freedom to choose residences would result in a scattering of Negro families throughout the entire urban area.

That many Negroes would continue to reside in areas of all-Negro concentration, even under circumstances that permit dispersion, would, in fact, make easier the dispersion process. Only a limited number of non-whites can afford, and wish, to move to white neighborhoods. This means that there could be a relatively complete dispersion of those so inclined, without their number becoming large in any single neighborhood.

The case of non-discrimination housing laws can best be argued in these terms. Such laws would allow the widespread dispersion of non-whites. Given the limited number of non-whites who would choose in the foreseeable future to take advantage of such laws, their main impact would be in preventing the kinds of concentration that frequently turn present "open occupancy" communities into crowded all-Negro slums.

Non-discriminatory laws, however, can do more harm than good unless they are enacted in large jurisdictions. The smallest effective area is probably a very large city. In smaller areas their effect might be to create the flight of white residents to "lily-white" jurisdictions. The full effect of non-discriminatory laws can be felt only if, in a given region, there are no such areas to which to flee. Even under this circumstance, laws against discrimination may produce a scattering of all-Negro residential pockets rather than genuine dispersions unless attempts are made to prevent the concentration of Negroes in any given neighborhood.

Panic flights of old-resident whites at the appearance of one or a few new-resident Negro families will be discouraged if the old residents know that, no matter where they move, a similar development might take place. The new residents in most cases will seek to avoid another all-Negro neighborhood. The interests of old and new residents become congruent on the points of maintaining neighborhood standards and mixed, rather than all-Negro, occupancy. Other less happy outcomes are of course possible. But non-discrimination laws, where combined with a sensitivity to the importance of not crowding Negroes into any single area, provide opportunities for giving Negroes the free residential choice they should have while simultaneously producing minimum disturbance in existing communities.

Controlled Migration

The case for non-discriminating laws thus rests largely on the point that they would filter non-whites in relatively small numbers to white communities. Laws of this sort are difficult to enforce. (How does one prove discrimination if a seller decides not to sell?)

Population groups are infinitely facile in frustrating unpopular laws. Public acceptance is necessary if interracial living is to be made possible.

The tipping phenomenon has meant that interracial communities in the United States (outside some slum areas) exist only where there also exist limits on the influx of nonwhites. In the usual case, these limits have been economic in nature. Thus the Kenwood region of Chicago is a truly interracial one. Homes in this neighborhood are large and expensive to maintain, and municipal housing codes are rigidly enforced. Pure economic pressures, combined with community acceptance of those Negroes who can afford to live there, have produced an upper-middle class interracial neighborhood.

In other cases, control of in-migration has been consciously contrived. The developers of the Philadelphia suburbs of Concord Park and Greenbelt Knoll have announced their intention of maintaining a white-Negro ratio of 55–45. Prospective purchasers place their names on a waiting list, and a purchase is made possible only if it maintains the desired racial distribution.

It is doubtful that many population groups, other than confirmed, egalitarian Quakers, would accept a ratio of Negroes at this high a point. On the other hand, Negro political leaders in the large cities could probably not remain political leaders if they were willing to accept controlled interracialism, set at a ratio that most whites would accept.

Nevertheless, experimentation with various systems of controlled migration is highly desirable. The tip-point phenomenon is so universal that it constitutes strong evidence in favor of control. Without control there has been a total failure to achieve interracial communities involving substantial numbers of Negroes anywhere in the great urban areas of America. Where controlled migration has been achieved, so has interracial living.

Many methods can be found to implement a controlled migration. A free real estate market, accompanied by enforced, adequate housing codes, is the preferred mechanism. The direct rationing of sales, as in the Philadelphia suburbs, is possible in a number of different forms. Community organizations of all types, including church groups, can be mobilized. Informal pressures upon real estate operators and mortgagers can be effective. The private, if not public, support of Negro leaders for controlled migration can be achieved. At Concord Park and Greenbelt Knoll, the builders found no opposition from Negroes to a balanced community pattern, once it was explained that the larger goal was to break down racial segregation. Many Negroes will support policies aimed at avoiding all-Negro communities if alternative housing opportunities are available.

The moral problem is not an easy one. It is the problem of placing limits upon Negro in-migration to particular urban and suburban areas. It means fostering a smaller discrimination in favor of scotching a larger one. Whatever the difficulties of such a position, it seems to be, for a large number of Negroes and whites alike, a preferable alternative to the present pattern of segregated population groups.

Returning White Population to Central Cities

Values of urbanism, other things being equal, compete easily with the suburban way of life. The other things now *not* equal include: modern, moderate priced housing; cleanliness and green space; good schools; safety against hoodlum attack; a sense of neighborhood solidarity. If such amenities were available, the attractions of urban life would almost certainly be sufficient to bring large numbers of white residents back into the cities. The cities offer a diversity of living conditions, a choice of companionship, and a range of leisure time activities that cannot be matched by the suburbs with their relatively closed and static conditions of life. The isolation of the dormitory suburbs, the large fraction of life demanded for commuting, and the social restriction of village living have already produced a swelling protest. Some segment of the metropolitan population is certainly composed of confirmed suburbanites, and no changes in the central city would attract them. But urban life would beckon large numbers if it could compete with suburbia in terms of the economics of housing, the safety and comfort of families, and the social solidarity of neighborhoods.

No precise data exist concerning the extent to which the disillusionment with the suburbs has already started a return flow to the cities. Certainly that flow has been considerable, especially among older couples, the more wealthy, and the childless. (The Chicago Gold Coast and the Manhattan luxury apartment would make important foci of research for measuring this flow.) What needs to be done is to bring into this stream the larger numbers of young and middle-aged couples who have families and who are not wealthy. Developments within the suburbs—the overcrowding of schools, the blighting of badly planned residential areas, and the full flowering of the uninhibited automobile culture—will provide an additional push toward the cities.

Whatever may be accomplished by individual home owners and real estate specialists will not be sufficient to reverse the massive population trends described earlier. The effort must be aided by governmental action. The important point is that governmental programs must be on a far larger scale than any action thus far undertaken.

The Metropolitan Area as a Racial Problem

The basic unit of operation must be a large site: a complete neighborhood or even a complete area of the city. The scale of urban renewal must be conceived not in square blocks, but in square miles. Destruction or rehabilitation of old urban dwellings and the building of new neighborhoods must be planned not in tens of acres but in hundreds. Whole sections of cities will have to be made over in order to attract an influx of stable white population groups.

Rebuilding on this scale is important for many reasons. And it would provide one opportunity to achieve interracial communities. Many white families affirm that they move to the suburbs not because they have Negroes for neighbors but because of the neighborhood deterioration that accompanies the high densities and rowdy behavior of the in-migrants. Large rebuilt areas, strictly controlled against over-crowding, would have the effect of removing such objections. Very large sums of public money will be required for this sort of program, but the obstacles are political rather than economic. Intricate collaborative devices among the local, state, and federal governments will be necessary. The history of urban redevelopment thus far, with few exceptions, is a history of too little, too late. Anything less than a massive program may have admirable local effects for particular population fractions, as when adequate housing is substituted for slum housing over several blocks for a few residents in New York's Harlem. These ameliorative programs are not to be criticized. But they do not attack the basic problem of the bifurcation of races on urban-suburban lines. To meet this problem, the rebuilding of entire sections of major cities is necessary.

The Suburbanization of Negroes

Any extensive rebuilding of central cities will displace Negro populations who inhabit the very urban areas most in need of rebuilding. No progress is possible unless a redistribution of the Negro population simultaneously occurs. One objective must be a migration of Negroes to suburban areas.

It is widely assumed that opening suburbs to Negroes would be readily achieved if there existed a single local government whose jurisdiction covered the entire metropolitan area. This is certainly too optimistic a view of the matter. Even under a metropolitan government, the people in outlying areas would not be without ability to resist, politically and socially, the incursion of what they consider "undesirable elements" into their communities. In Chicago and in many other places, residents of "better" neighborhoods *within* the central city have successfully opposed housing measures which threatened to bring Negro residents into their areas. If the free distribution of non-white groups is not politically feasible on an inter-neighborhood basis, the creation of a metropolitan government will certainly not make it so on an inter-city one. A single government for a whole area might conceivably provide a more satisfactory political arena for the eventual solution of distributing non-white groups throughout an entire metropolitan area, but will not *ipso facto* guarantee that distribution.

Nor is it true that restrictions on the migration of Negro and other non-white groups to the suburbs is solely a class or economic matter. Any examination of the variety of suburban conditions leads to the conclusion that urban blight and the dilapidated housing and social conditions that accompany it are not uniquely characteristic of the central cities. Rather, blight exists in varying degrees of intensity in all parts of the metropolitan area, central city and suburbs alike. In all but the very newest of planned suburban developments, many dwelling units exist which, in the terms of the Bureau of the Census, "should be torn down, extensively repaired, or rebuilt." Only a fraction of these units are Negro dwellings. In many metropolitan areas a larger proportion of dwelling units outside than inside the central city are dilapidated or lack running water.

Despite these facts, in many suburban areas the extravagances of legal restrictions covering suburban building should be examined for their effect upon maintaining Negro urban concentrations. Provisions covering lot sizes, sidewalks, streets, building setbacks, and building materials often have very little to do with the maintenance of standards of health and decency. They are, rather, frankly established to stabilize or to upgrade community levels, including the maintenance of their racial character. The effect is to make suburban housing too expensive for even the Negroes who otherwise could afford, and would prefer, suburban living. Less extravagant building and housing codes would certainly lead to some greater degree of Negro suburbanization. This can be accomplished without producing additional suburban slums. The antidote to overstringent building restrictions is not their complete abolition.

Non-discriminatory housing laws would, as we have seen, go a long way in encouraging some suburbanization of Negroes. Other discriminating practices—many of them extra-legal—should be ended. If local building inspectors cannot be trained to administer laws impartially, they should be replaced by officials who can, under state or federal supervision. If local police forces will not protect the property and lives of Negro purchasers of suburban homes, then procedures for training, replacing, or penalizing such officials must be adopted. If established realtors will not sell to Negroes, others should be encouraged, and perhaps paid, to do so.

Social attitudes change more slowly than laws, and only a moderate incursion of Negroes into established suburbs can be expected in the near future. The best chance for even this modest development is under community auspices on the basis of controlled migrations. The need for Negro suburban housing will greatly exceed the receptivity of the established suburbs, especially if central city rebuilding is undertaken on the scale that it is needed. This sharply raises the question of the desirability of encouraging all-Negro suburbs.

The negative consideration is obvious: all-Negro suburbs would simply substitute one sort of segregated life for another. On the other hand, there is much to be said on the positive side. Such suburbs would be a large factor in redressing the present imbalance in the urban-suburban population distribution. As we have seen, this in itself is a highly desirable step. Secondly, such communities, adequately planned and constructed, would provide a great improvement in living conditions, superior to both the urban and suburban slums in which so large a proportion of Negroes now reside. Thirdly, and perhaps most importantly, the all-Negro middle-class suburb could very well constitute a significant step in the direction of large-scale interracial communities. Present conditions of life of the largest fraction of the Negro population discourage, rather than encourage, the habits of thought and conduct deemed desirable by the larger white community. The middle-class Negro suburb would foster such attributes. If class, in addition to skin color, is a principal cause of segregation, then the class differential may be overcome by the middle-class suburban life.

As in so many planned social changes, schemes for all-Negro suburban communities may produce unexpected ill consequences. One deserves mention. Grant the truth of what has been said: that good suburban housing in a good suburban neighborhood will aid in producing a Negro population of model, middle-class, social attributes, and that nothing distinguishes this group from middle-class whites except skin color. It is then easily assumed that interracial living is the next step. But the opposite assumption must also be entertained: that whites will continue to resist interracial living. In this event Negroes will all the more resent their segregation and whites will have no line except the color line on which to take a stand. If Negro-white tensions pivot exclusively on color, they may be exacerbated to a new point of bitterness.

Despite such dangers, the more persuasive evidence is that Negro-white tensions will decrease, not increase, as the populations become socially more alike. For this reason, as well as the need to meet short-run housing requirements, experiments with all-Negro suburban communities should be encouraged.

Negroes to Smaller Cities

Discussion of the possible distribution of some Negroes to points outside the larger metropolitan areas does not fall strictly within the purposes of this study. Yet it is worth noting that Negroes are greatly underrepresented in virtually all places outside the South and the larger urban areas of the rest of the country. A program of encouraging migration to these smaller cities would somewhat mitigate the large city, urban-suburban racial bifurcation and, at the same time, establish important new opportunities for integrated living. The effects of such an effort should not be overestimated. For example, if one unrealistically assumes it were possible for non-southern cities of from 10 thousand to 250 thousand population to be increased 5 per cent in total population by an in-migration of Negroes, the total number so placed would be about a million, or less than the number of Negroes in New York City at the 1960 census.

Nevertheless, attempts to locate Negroes in cities of this

size—as well as in smaller urban areas—would be worth-while. Since employment opportunities in industry consti-tute the most important attraction for Negro in-migrants, the success of such attempts would pivot upon the avail-ability of such jobs for Negroes (therefore a shortage of white workers) and upon information concerning such op-portunities being disseminated among potential migrants. The former factor will to a large extent depend upon fur-ther industrial growth in small- and medium-size urban areas. The factor of publicity is more immediately con-trollable. The information flow now directed at potential migrants from the South (by such organizations as the Urban League) could very well be focused more sharply on the existing and emerging opportunities outside the larger metropolitan areas.

No single measure will solve the problem in any single area, and the same combination of measures will not be appropriate as leverage points in any two areas. What strikes the observer is the paucity of imagination that has been brought to bear on the issue. The Quaker communi-ties in the Philadelphia area provide a model for one kind of controlled migration that is only slowly being taken up in other places. The investment in almost any city of, say, a million dollars in a revolving fund for the purchase of homes to foster interracial neighborhoods, with careful planning and public relations, could make a dent in the pattern of segregation. A well-staffed, resourceful office with the objective of publicizing successes of interracial residential contacts would be a valuable positive aid to enlarging those contacts and no less valuable a means of dissipating images of disagreeableness and violence that widely prevail.

Action programs of this sort are obvious needs. Beyond them there exists a wide range of more experimental possibilities for both private and public agencies. For example, there are a number of newly built areas in the central cities whose attractiveness and proximity to work and recreational facilities make them highly desirable living places. Lake Meadows, in Chicago, is a good example of this sort of development. Nevertheless, these areas tend to become all-Negro communities because of their relatively small size, or their situation close to older Negro slums, or other factors. It might be possible to make such newly built areas model interracial neighborhoods. How can white residents be attracted to them? A private foundation might bring the attractions of such developments to the attention of whites by maintaining a good small museum at such a site or by arranging concerts there (but at no other nearby place) of outstanding musical groups, or by providing superior park and swimming facilities, or indeed by partially subsidizing rental costs for limited periods. The marginal attractions needed to bring whites into such intrinsically attractive areas may in many cases be quite small; and once a pattern of interracial living is successfully achieved it may be expected to continue as subsidies are diminished. Private organizations could in a similar way reward suburban communities that make it easy for Negroes to take up residence.

The national government may not be barred from an analogous type of activity. A good case can be made for a federal program to provide suburbs with aid for community facilities they already need and will need even more in years to come: schools, parks, libraries, swimming pools, and similar amenities. It is commonplace for federal legislation to establish conditions that must be met by local governments before they qualify for financial aid. The question arises: is it possible to write a federal law that would supply aid for community facilities on a priority basis to those suburbs containing a given minimum of Negro residents? Constitutional and political questions immediately arise. Clearly no requirement based directly upon a racial classification would meet constitutional standards. Yet it is not beyond the realm of legal creativity to find another scheme of definition that would foster the end of racial distribution and yet remain within constitutional limits. The more difficult objection is political, but it is by no means insurmountable. Even southern congressmen might support such a measure if for no other reason than glee over the embarrassment of their northern colleagues. The larger point is not to argue for the desirability or feasibility of this particular measure, but rather to suggest the need for inventive action. The growing consequences of the population schism, plus the plight that many suburbs will soon find themselves in, combine to bring within the realm of probability even schemes that at first blush seem impossible of achievement.

The whole discussion of "solutions" now rests too largely upon moral terms. The wealth of the United States has historically been used to remove issues from the idealistic to a cash basis, and in this issue, too, cash may be a great salve for moral wounds. This is not meant to be a cynical statement. It is, rather, counsel for the strategy of induced social change. Payment in the form of needed community facilities should accompany other types of action.

Church, social work, and educational institutions must prepare the ground for interracial living and must be ready to act when tensions occur. Indeed, mobilization of resources must take place over a very wide range, from training police officers in problems of race relations to the establishment of special community programs for the improvement of interracial contacts; from the provision of social services for Negro in-migrants to education programs for prospective employers of Negroes; from block activity preparing the way for Negro neighbors to nation-wide programs that implement basic Negro civil rights. Every community facility—churches, schools, labor unions, recreational groups, economic organizations, and government—can be enlisted. Here, as with almost all programs of civic change, working through established institutions and existing voluntary groups is the best avenue to success.

VII. CONCLUSION

It is frequently argued that problems created by the present distribution of Negroes in the large metropolitan areas are only transitory problems. They will solve themselves through the normal processes of acculturation. This view holds that every immigrant wave to the great cities has at least initially produced disadvantaged ethnic islands. With the passage of time, however, these islands have given way as the second and third generations have acquired cultural characteristics of the larger society and broken away from the habits of conduct of their immigrant fathers and grandfathers. This is the pattern of the Jews in New York, the Poles in Chicago, the Italians in San Francisco. There is some evidence that the Negro group is going through the same process as its members surmount social, vocational, professional, and residential barriers. All the problem needs is time. The American melting pot will work for Negroes as it has for others.

This is a hopeful view. Despite many examples of successful interracial adjustment, it is a view not substantiated by either history or available data. The example of earlier European immigrants all concern white populations. No statistically significant evidence exists indicating the inevitable dissolution of the Negro concentrations. As with Japanese-Americans before World War II, acceptance by the larger community for a relatively few Negroes is being accompanied by life within closed communities for the relatively many. (The Japanese community in Los Angeles grew continuously between 1900 and 1942.) The factor of skin color, alone, is one cause for the different course of development. The very size of the Negro concentration in the larger cities, resulting in the establishment of an entire Negro economic and social life, can also be expected to obstruct the decline of the communities in which that life flourishes. To this must be added the disinclination of many white groups to accept Negroes as neighbors and social companions. The total picture for the future, if present trends are unaltered, is the further breaking down of some boundaries of the closed community affecting proportionately small numbers of Negroes. For the largest numbers, segregation will continue and probably increase, rather than decline.

This is almost certainly the correct prognosis for the immediate 30 years ahead. To the extent that the natural acculturation argument is one covering the distant future —say 80 or 100 years—it may have greater accuracy. But to that extent it is largely irrelevant. The central cities of the metropolitan areas dominate the nation not only in population but also in retail and wholesale sales, manufacturing, and the provision of services to individuals and businesses. They set the tone and pattern for the entire complex of community interdependence in politics, economics, and cultural life. If the analysis presented here is accurate, the whole nation is faced with a wide range of deleterious consequences. And these consequences will take their toll long before the "natural desuetude" of segregation is accomplished. This is the justification for taking all positive steps possible to end the present patterns of segregation.

Another reason for not disturbing the current population distribution might lie in the danger that dispersion would deprive Negroes of the political power they have acquired as the consequence of concentration. This is not a valid argument for two reasons.

On the one hand, it does not take into account the genuine gains that accrue to the Negro population as the consequence of dispersion. Increasing strain in race relations seems always to accompany concentrated numbers. Where a minority group is dispersed, it is less visible, less likely to be considered a unit, less feared, less subject to discrimination. Where it is concentrated and segregated, it is more likely to be relegated to a subordinate position, and its members have fewer opportunities for assimilation into the larger social structure.

On the other hand, dispersion of residential areas would not necessarily lead to a decline in Negro political power. The 100 per cent Negro voting districts can be viewed as a type of gerrymandering in which political power is lost by the very concentration of voters. Negroes consituting 50 per cent of the voters in two election districts (or 25 per cent in four districts) will wield more political power than if they composed 100 per cent of a single district. What is to be avoided is the halfway house: not enough dispersion to prevent clear subordination, with not enough concentration to make numbers politically effective. Within the larger metropolitan areas this is an unlikely possibility. The gains to be made by Negroes from political action built upon concentration can never equal those that can be achieved by dispersion throughout the metropolitan areas.

The programs suggested for overcoming Negro concentrations face great obstacles. They arouse the ire of the ignorant and the prejudiced. They are disquieting to even the fair-minded and the sophisticated who live good lives and who perform their civic duties conscientiously. And they will be bitterly opposed by a wide range of people: owners, mortgagers, and others who profit from the present patterns of land use; political leaders in the central cities, including Negro leaders, who fear the dissipation of established constituencies, as well as political leaders of other areas whose tenure will be disturbed by the incursion of new voters into their districts; old residents of suburbs and the better central-city neighborhoods who hold strongly to their comfortable social situations and established shopping, social, and educational patterns. Even those with humanitarian motives will voice opposition to some plans on the grounds that they constitute an unwarranted interference in the life patterns of the poor. And Negro groups and leaders will not easily be won over to some aspects of the proposed program. They will, for example, see large-scale urban renewal as a displacement and an imposition, before its advantages will be apparent. Negroes have already in many cities distinguished themselves for their opposition to smaller-scale programs of urban renewal. Some of this opposition may be blunted, as when Negro opposition to urban renewal is placated by well-planned programs of relocation housing. But every such move, in turn, is likely to increase opposition from other sources, in the example given from areas in which the relocation housing is to be placed.

Despite difficulties and despite the uncertainty of success, all efforts are justified. The stakes are high: the preservation and further development of many facets of urban American life, for whites and Negroes alike. By building a non-discriminatory housing market in both city and suburbs, income and social attributes, not race, can be maximized as the criteria for residential location. By rebuilding large areas of central cities, white populations can be induced to return to those cities. By combating restrictions against Negro occupancy of suburbs, a flow of non-whites can be started in that direction. By attracting Negroes to jobs in the smaller cities outside the South, where they are now underrepresented, some of the present and potential city-suburban population imbalance may be corrected. By encouraging through community resources the controlled migration of Negroes into all areas of city and suburbs, a significant redistribution of Negroes and whites can take place. All these measures minimize the dangerous operation of the tip-point psychology. Here, as elsewhere, nothing succeeds like success, and a demonstration that such a program can produce results in one metropolitan area of the nation will be important for all areas. The only way to avoid the consequences of racial schism is to bridge it.

Can Intergroup Quotas Be Benign?

DAN W. DODSON

For those concerned with intergroup relations, one of the most baffling problems is that of engineering desegregation programs so that ratios among different peoples are maintained in such proportions that the weight of numbers of one group does not constitute a threat to the other.

Most would concede that there is a relation between proportion of those to be integrated and the successful attempt to maintain stabilized relations in the desegregated groups. We are not too sure what other factors are involved, however.

In the high school situation in New York City the experience seems to be that, as the percentage of Negroes in the student population approaches 30, the white group starts to withdraw *en masse*. When the white pupils start withdrawing, the better students of the Negro group also leave, so that the school is left with a greatly reduced student body, frequently composed of youngsters with various problems of adjustment. One school (Wadleigh) had to be closed as a high school because of such a development. Two others (Benjamin Franklin and Boys High in Brooklyn) are rapidly facing similar predicaments. There may be others which are unknown to this writer.

At the neighborhood level, the elementary schools make out better. Here proportions of Negroes to whites seem to make little difference up to and well beyond the 50 per cent point. Stable and sustained mixed elementary school populations are achieved in most neighborhoods with little difficulty.

Seeley reported in *Crestwood Heights* that when the Jewish population started migrating into the community they were widely and warmly accepted. When they became an identifiable and self-conscious group the relations between them and the other population became more formal. When their numbers had grown to one-fourth of the total, hostility and conflict ensued; around the 35 per cent point, large-scale withdrawal of the Christian group started.

Racial Quotas in Housing

A theory of benign quotas is being tested in residential housing by the Milgrim Associates in their projects. The assumption is that whites do not mind living with Negro neighbors provided they can be assured that the values of the dominant group will not be "drowned" by the number of Negroes. Hence there is a consciously established quota system in which some houses are held off the white market to assure that some Negroes are accommodated.

The controversy over this bold venture has not subsided. Deerfield Park in Illinois has been torn by strife over it. Intergroup relations leaders in public agencies who have to enforce fair housing laws and public policies have privately expressed concern over what they would do should a complaint be filed against such a developer who discriminated in his attempt to achieve some semblance of balance in the racial backgrounds of residents in such projects.

In New York City, as in many other communities, the question is asked increasingly: what can be done with public housing to keep it integrated? Many whites are reluctant to live in projects with Negroes—especially if Negroes are in the majority. Likewise, many Negroes do not want to live in projects where they are a small minority—especially if they have to live long distances from the Negro communities to do so. Also in many of the City projects, sometimes referred to as "low middle income," fewer Negroes than whites can afford the rentals.

There is a backlog of applications amounting to some 67,000, composed mainly of Negro and Puerto Rican families, for public housing in New York. What should be the responsibility of the public authority to *seek* eligible continental whites to move into the projects to help maintain interracial balances? A few years back, one leader openly advocated formal quotas in one project in the Bronx as a means of maintaining a stable racial balance.

Private volunteer organizations face a like problem. The new group in a changing neighborhood tends to be Negro or Puerto Rican. If the agency serves needs it concentrates heavily on the minority groups. If it values integration of all peoples, it invariably reaches the place where it must pass over some of the minority constituency in order to hold the majority group. This is discrimination.

The problem is not new, either in philosophy or practice. What is new is the changing relationship of groups to each other.

"COLOR-BLIND" DICTUM

The basic philosophy of intergroup relations in crashing through institutionalized segregation and *apartheid* policies was most clearly stated by Justice Harlan in the famous *Plessy v. Ferguson* decision. In his dissent he stated that any arm of government in dealing with people should be "color blind."

"Without regard to race, creed or color" has been the phraseology of all anti-bias laws so far enacted. Obviously such legislation was targeted to the abolition of institutionalized Jim Crow. Its objective was to destroy formal policies of discrimination. In this context we were not satisfied with "tokenism" as a philosophy. The fight on college quotas suggests that token integration as an institutionalized policy is unsatisfactory. The complaint of the South today is over "token" integration. We all deplore the policy of the agency which employs one Negro and places him in a prominent spot as evidence of integration. We refer to such a person as "Exhibit A."

In this first phase of desegregation, Harlan's statement and the phraseology of the law has been of tremendous importance. In New York City the first housing authority administrator was able to get integrated housing because he said: "This is public housing. Being public it is available to all the public who qualify, without regard to race, creed or color." In a like measure the laws against discrimination have said: "You do not have to employ a man on any other basis than before, except that race, creed or color shall not be a factor in determining his qualifications."

Today, however, when it comes to integration as contrasted to desegregation, the shoe is on the other foot. The Supreme Court decision in May 1954 can be, and is, widely interpreted to mean that children reared in segregation are traumatized in their perception of self. This has injected a new value into the picture. This value indicates that when segregation, either enforced or *de facto*, occurs it is the responsibility of government to use positive means to break it up. This cannot be done by being color blind.

ACHIEVING INTERGROUP BALANCE

On the other hand, to take race into account in employment, housing (in New York), public accommodations, or education would be a violation of the law. Thus the means used to achieve the objective of stable, integrated racial balances appear to be at variance with the present anti-discrimination laws, especially if public agencies are involved.

Another limitation to the honest evaluation of the situation is our paucity of knowledge about such group problems. All would concede that there is nothing magic about a percentage of 30 or 40 or any other. The use of such a number becomes dangerous because it reinforces stereotypes about what such proportions should be and limits experimentation on how to deal with the many other variables.

Undoubtedly another variable is that of the climate in which the groups interact. There are some instances in which whites have come into Negro-majority situations and remained. It should be pointed out that the whites began as an infinitesimally small minority and ultimately took over the Georgetown section in Washington, D.C. A racially balanced neighborhood was achieved in the Bolton Hill section of Baltimore in a comparable way. Another factor is that of the nature of the group. A task-oriented group undoubtedly would respond differently to one that was socially oriented.

Another factor related to achieving stabilized intergroup balances is the weight of a historical past. For instance, an agency which refuses to integrate as a neighborhood changes, frequently finds itself surrounded by minority group persons. Integration becomes a *cause celebre* in some such instances. Hence, when the color line is ultimately broken, it is like the bursting of a dam which has held back pent-up waters. In such instances too often nothing can be done to keep racial balance.

The next question to be raised is: "How effective are quotas, anyway?" If the agency is facing rapid neighborhood change, usually they have little effect. There are some who would say that when imaginative volunteer leadership cannot succeed in holding integrated groups there is no hope for quotas unless there is resort to coercion.

OTHER MEANS TO SAME END

Before serious consideration is given to formal quotas, all other means of achieving balance should be exhausted. What are these? One is selection through program emphasis. Sometimes it is possible to maintain racial balance through programming. The Bronx High School of Science fulfills this purpose. The reason the high school division has moved from comprehensive schools to such special schools is due, in no small part, to this problem of racial and ethnic mixing.

A second type of alternative is selective recruitment. This is particularly useful for some types of agencies. The housing authority personnel can seek assistance from local organizations to get qualified persons of select backgrounds to apply. A dean of a popular college told me once that he could fill his entire freshman class from Brooklyn without lowering his admission standards and 95 per cent of the new students would be Jewish. This led to selective recruitment and regional quotas rather than racial quotas. Some of the private schools which are heavily homogeneous in enrollment are extremely generous with scholarships for those of other backgrounds in order to keep some integration and the practice is defined for precisely the same reason as the court ruled, i.e., segregated education is *ipso facto* inferior.

Another device is school districting or other policy programs. In public education zoning for racial balance holds many possibilities. For example, Princeton, New Jersey, integrated the schools by sending the first three grades to one building and the other grades to the second school plant. This mixed the children and provided wholesome integration. The proposed New Rochelle plan for a K-3 (kindergarten through third grade) school in the Negro community and the distribution of the older children in schools outside the Negro district is suggestive.

ARE QUOTAS JUSTIFIED?

After all the possibilities are exhausted, however, there is still this issue: "Can racial quotas be justified? If so, under what circumstances?"

Few of us are doctrinaire on this issue. For official, i.e., public agencies, I would say, no! I well realize there are great traumas to personality of both Negroes and whites stemming from what has been a historical past. These biases make it difficult to achieve an integrated community. I have very much sympathy for public officials who are experimenting with programs designed to achieve mixed groups in public agencies. Their objectives are good. I have not been able to bring myself to an endorsement of such a program, however.

With 67,000 applicants for public housing, for instance, and many of these consisting of families of several members living in one room, it is hard to endorse holding an apartment vacant hoping some one with a white skin will apply and pass by those in such need.

If such programs of benign quotas are launched it appears that the following points should be clear:

(1) What are the criteria by which one establishes what the quota should be? 20 per cent, 30 per cent, 90, etc.

(2) Can such a quota be defended as an interim or "phase" operation? There is the assumption here that all desire a society where, ultimately, there is free association of peoples, yet, when quotas are established they tend to become "frozen," institutionalized and difficult to change.

(3) How are the "weightings" established by which

"desegregation" as a value transcends "non-discrimination" as a value? It should be noted that unless there is "discrimination" there is little problem.

(4) How can the "phase operation" be terminated when it has outlived its usefulness? Once social structure is created it tends to resist change.

(5) Are we sure we are not injecting our own values to deprive even minority people of their right to self-segregation? Does this threaten the entire pattern of grouping around social and religious interests? For example, in one neighborhood in New Rochelle over 90 per cent of the children in the school are Jewish in background. These are homes of the $40,000 class. Most such upper-income people could have chosen—with some search—more integrated neighborhoods in which to live. Does such a policy of quota programming deny this privilege?

Private agencies are in a less vulnerable position, although they too face the dilemma that—pushed too far—quotas mean discrimination. Where such measures are employed it should be clear, even here, that there is an element of experiment in it; that there are clearly delineated procedures for sharing the fruits of the experiment with others.

THE TASK AHEAD

In summation, my position is as follows: (1) As we move beyond *desegregation* toward integration, we move away from Justice Harlan's position on the role of government as regards race, creed and color. (2) Public and private agencies both must take into account race or creed if creative roles are to be developed and maintained.

This "due regard for race or creed" cannot, however, be used as an excuse to resort to preferential treatment of people because of race, creed or color. In such areas as housing and education, where weighting of variables includes the need for mixed association as a social value, it should be very clear how and in what way this value takes precedence over the need for service as a value. Perhaps the establishment of these weights is the next task ahead.

Is "Integration" Possible in the New York Schools?

NATHAN GLAZER

One way or another, "integration" has become an important issue in every Northern and Western city in which there are large numbers of Negroes and (as in New York) Puerto Ricans or (in California and elsewhere) Mexicans. The constellation of forces and problems is different in each situation. But what happens in New York is important enough by itself; here is the city with the largest population in the country, the largest number of Negroes, the largest number of Puerto Ricans. The New York school system has well over 800 elementary schools, junior high and high schools. It comprises about a million students, has 45 thousand employees and spends 400 million dollars a year. Sixty new school buildings were opened in the three years 1957–59.

These dazzling figures indicate that there can be no comparison between New York's school problems and those of a community with, let us say, a half dozen schools, where citizens are in direct control of school planning through their power to elect school board officials, to approve or disapprove bond issues, and the like. In such a community, the citizen voting on a bond issue for a new school knows in advance just where the school will be, and what effect if any its location will have on segregating or integrating Negro students; such knowledge presumably plays a role in how the vote goes. So, for example, in

Malverne, Long Island, when a school bond issue for a new school was voted down, the outcome was seen as a defeat for segregation—though conceivably other issues were involved.

There can be no such clear-cut victories and defeats in New York City. Perhaps in frustration, many people act as if New York were Malverne, and as if some single decision on zoning, or school building, or teacher placement would radically transform the educational system. The matter, unfortunately, is not so simple.

The story begins with the Supreme Court decision of May 17, 1954, outlawing segregation. What was involved, of course, was the formal and legal segregation of the Southern and Border states. However, a month later, Professor Kenneth Clark of City College, a psychologist whose studies on the development of Negro children in the South had played a role in the Supreme Court decision, asserted: "It would be a mistake to assume that the content and spirit of the . . . decision apply only to the Southern states that have laws which require segregation. As I understand the decision, the United States Supreme Court has clearly stated that segregation itself damages the personality of human beings. The court did not limit itself to the statement that only legal segregation is detrimental to the human personality. It was explicit . . . in stating that various forms of racial segregation are damaging to the human spirit. . . ."

There is of course no formal segregation in the New York City schools. But there are great numbers of Negroes and Puerto Ricans in certain areas—concentrations which partly exist because these groups meet discrimination in their efforts to rent or buy houses in many other sections of the city. For despite a city ordinance forbidding it, discrimination in housing is still widespread, and in any case the residential patterns created by it still persist. These concentrations have an equally important cause in the poverty of Negroes and Puerto Ricans, a fact which automatically eliminates the great majority of them from large sections of the city. Finally, the Negro and Puerto Rican concentrations have a happier, positive aspect, reflecting ties to family, friends, institutions—a community.

Professor Clark opened the integration issue in New York schools in the wake of the Supreme Court decision. He spoke of segregation in the North as well as in the South—and there is no question that there are 100 per cent Negro and 100 per cent white schools in the North, as in the South. But there is a decisive difference between the two situations. Because segregation is *legally* imposed in the South, and because the whole tendency of the American creed opposes legal distinctions made between human beings of different races and ethnic groups, it is necessary to strike down segregation in the Southern schools on moral and political grounds, independently of any effect such separation might have on education. Even if the Southern states had given superior education to Negroes in their separate schools (and in their frantic efforts to bring up the miserably poor quality of Negro schooling to avoid a negative Supreme Court ruling, many Southern states were beginning to spend a good deal more on Negro schools), it would still have been necessary to abolish this legal separation by public authority.

But in the North the concentration of Negroes and whites into separate schools was the effect of other social forces. There was no claim by Northern political bodies that they had any moral or political right to enforce such a separation. The situation was similar to the concentration of Jews in the schools of the Lower East Side in 1910, or of Italians in the schools of "Little Italy" around the same time. I emphasize this difference between the Northern and Southern states because I think the application of the term "segregation" to both introduces a radical confusion. In a word, the difference is: Southern segregation has to be abolished *independently* of its impact on education; Northern school concentration becomes a problem that demands action primarily *because* it may lead to inferior education for Negro children.

If the concentration of Negroes in certain Northern schools were not simply the product of their residential concentration, and if school zones were gerrymandered by political authorities so as to increase the separation of Negro and white children, then the situation would be comparable to that in the South. Indeed many observers believed this to be the case in New York City; it is certainly the case in other Northern places. But Professor Clark raised only the question of the quality of education that Negro children were getting or could get in Northern de facto "segregated" schools. And the day after Professor Clark's speech, the president of the Board of Education of New York City requested the Public Education Association to investigate the status of the education of Negro and Puerto Rican children in the city.

The report was submitted a year later. It compared schools with a high concentration of Negroes and Puerto Ricans (more than 90 per cent Negro and Puerto Rican if they were elementary schools, more than 85 per cent Negro and Puerto Rican if they were junior high schools), with schools with a low concentration of Negroes and Puerto Ricans (less than 10 per cent Negro and Puerto Rican). There were then 49 of these high-concentration schools—somewhat less than 10 per cent of the total number of schools in the city. (It should also be pointed out that only about a third of the Negro and Puerto Rican children in the city attended these high-concentration schools.) The comparison proved interesting.

It turned out that while slightly less was spent on the education of children in the high-concentration elementary schools than those in the other schools ($185 to $195 per child), the situation was reversed in the junior high schools ($252 per child in the high-concentration schools, $244 per child in the other schools). The professional staffs in the high-concentration schools were larger, indicating the need for, and the supply of, more special services. Thus in the high-concentration elementary schools, there were 25.8 children per professional position, in the other elementary schools, 28.7; in the high-concentration junior high schools, 19.4 children per professional position, in the others, 22.7.

Two objective indices stamped the schools with high proportions of Negroes and Puerto Ricans as being inferior: they were on the average older (43 years as against 31 years for the elementary schools; 35 as against 15 years for the junior high schools). And there were fewer regular teachers in the high-concentration schools, more substitute teachers.

On the crucial question of zoning, the report stated that no attempted "equalization" of Negro-Puerto Rican and "other" children seemed to play any role in setting up zones, nor did any attempt to keep the groups separate play any such role. It asserted: "There is no significant evidence to indicate that ethnic separation is seriously considered in drawing school district boundary lines."

At this point, the Board of Education might well have said, well, that's that. We spend as much on the Negro and Puerto Rican children as we do on the others; we give them more services; if their schools are older, this is an unfortunate consequence of the fact that they live in older neighborhoods; and if they are inferior in academic achievement (as they were), this is owing to lower I.Q.'s, language difficulties, poor home environment, and the host

139

of factors, known and unknown, that differentiate children of different backgrounds in academic achievement. Indeed, when one looks at this report, the only conceivable legitimate ground for complaint was to be found in the distribution of regular teachers. Some of the more skeptical among us might even wonder whether the older, regular teachers, would do any better with Negro and Puerto Rican children, than the younger "substitutes" (who in effect are regular employees, with full teaching loads, but without the teacher's license, which is often dependent on meeting the requirements imposed by the teaching guild, requirements whose relation to teaching ability is open to question). But here was a point at which, if more regular teachers meant improvement, then improvement, despite the difficulties of shifting older, established teachers with tenure, was possible.

But we must separate the issue of "segregation" from that of education: regardless of what the study showed as to the *education* of Negro and Puerto Rican children, the fact remained that large numbers of them were in schools with very few continental white children—and this was, in terms of political impact, the real issue. The president of the Board of Education is a political appointee; even if he were not, the head of an enterprise of the size of the New York City schools would have to keep political realities continually in mind. Even before the report of the Public Education Association was presented, it was decided that something must be done to integrate the New York schools further, and a Commission on Integration was set up. Subcommissions worked on the problems of educational standards and curriculum: Guidance; Educational Stimulation and Placement; Teachers Assignment and Personnel; Community Relations and Information; Zoning; and Physical Plant and Maintenance. The individual subcommission reports were submitted to the Board between March 1956 and June 1957; the final report was submitted in July 1958. And now, two years later, we have a huge progress report: "Toward Greater Opportunity," subtitled "A Progress Report from the Superintendent of Schools to the Board of Education Dealing with Implementation of Recommendations of the Commission on Integration."

The crux of the matter politically has always been, and still remains, zoning. The Board of Education, despairing over effecting any really satisfying changes through zoning, keeps on emphasizing programs to raise the level of education and services in schools that will have to remain largely Puerto Rican and Negro. But this does not get it off the political hook. It is caught in the dilemma of a political demand that is simple and clear—no all-Negro schools—but a demand which it cannot meet since the huge residential concentrations of Negroes and Puerto Ricans in effect must mean many largely Puerto Rican and Negro schools.

And despite laws against residential and occupational discrimination, which should serve to upgrade the economic level of Puerto Ricans and Negroes, and spread them more evenly through the city, the situation cannot undergo any great change. For—and this is the most striking and important fact in the report on the progress of integration—*three-quarters* of the school children of Manhattan are Negro and Puerto Rican; *two-fifths* of the school children of greater New York are Negro and Puerto Rican.[1] If by an elaborate process of busing and pupil assignment it were possible to evenly distribute the Negro

---

[1] The disproportionate number of Negro and Puerto Rican children in New York schools can be explained not only by differential family sizes, but also by the fact that an estimated one third of Manhattan school children, mostly white, attend private schools.

and Puerto Rican children throughout the city—taking the children of Brooklyn into Queens, the children from Manhattan into the Bronx, and then alternatively bringing the children of the Bronx and Queens into Brooklyn and Manhattan, etc., etc.—then Negro and Puerto Rican children would make up two-fifths of the total in every school in the city.

But even this theoretically perfect situation could not be maintained for long—the numbers of Negro and Puerto Rican children in the city are increasing rapidly. The Puerto Rican birth rate is much higher than the Negro birth rate, which is higher than the white birth rate. Migratory trends are harder to estimate, but it is certain that Negro and Puerto Rican increase through immigration, and white decrease through out-migration, will continue. In effect, the notion that much would be accomplished by the redistribution of a declining number of continental white school children is an illusion.

Meanwhile, no one—including the Board of Education—has offered evidence that there is any relation at all between the educational outcome, for Negroes and Puerto Ricans, and schools in which they form 80 or 90 per cent of the population, as against schools in which they make up 40 per cent of the population. All this leaves aside the question of whether the educational outcome for "other" children in schools where these "others" form a minority or half of the school population is worse than in schools in which they form 80 or 90 per cent of the school population. We may, for all we know, be facing one of those dilemmas in which the improvement of the education of Negro and Puerto Rican children through redistribution is accompanied by a poorer educational outcome for white children. But on this question our knowledge is a complete blank.

Meanwhile, despite the absence of any data, the Board

of Education has taken the position that an even mixture of groups is educationally desirable—that, to quote the resolution setting up the Commission on Integration, "racially homogeneous schools are undesirable." This means all-white as well as all-Negro schools. And the report before us indicates how extended have been the Board's efforts to promote such an even distribution.

While the Board considers distribution in the siting of new schools, the change in population is so rapid, and length of time between planning and opening so great, that very often a school planned for a fringe area, for heterogeneity, opens up finally in a mostly Negro or Puerto Rican area. The Board also considers distribution in setting up zones for old schools; but, as we have indicated, and to put it crudely, there are generally not enough "other" children to go around. The battles that take place between principals and parent groups of various schools over the relatively small numbers of continental white children would be comic—if they were not rather pitiful. And in the end, any victories are likely to be Pyrrhic ones. The assignment of a few blocks containing fifty "other" children to a school that is largely Negro and Puerto Rican does not necessarily mean an increase by fifty in the number of "other" children. Maybe only ten or twenty will show up when school opens, and the battle will have been in vain. There are always alternatives for resisting parents—parochial and private schools (which enroll one-third of the children of school age in New York City); or the move to the suburbs—precipitated, perhaps, by the zoning change.

The Board of Education is unhappily aware of all these problems. If rezoning cannot accomplish much, a certain amount of redistributing of the school population can be done by busing. A thousand children from the heavily Negro Bedford-Stuyvesant area of Brooklyn are bused to schools in Queens and Brooklyn, and another 400 are bused from Harlem to Yorkville in Manhattan. While overcrowding in some schools and under-utilization in others has been in the past publicly given as the reason for such moves (to quiet agitated parents and community groups), the report of the Commission does include such busing schemes as part of the over-all integration efforts of the schools.

But the major problem is still: the poor educational results for Negroes and Puerto Ricans. And here is where the chief efforts of the Board of Education have been applied. One can only say, they are impressive in their scale.

The fact is that the needs of Negro and Puerto Rican children are enormous. Very large numbers come from homes in which they receive no care, are not fed properly, are perhaps abused physically and psychologically. The school may be a haven—but more likely it is another area in which a depressed and miserable existence is reflected in apathy, outrageous behavior, resistance. Obviously these are not problems peculiar to Negroes or Puerto Ricans—but equally obviously, the highest incidence of such problems occurs in that part of the city's population. All this is aside from special factors affecting the two groups that bear directly on the capacity to learn. In the Puerto Rican case, there is the serious language problem. In 1958, 62,000 children were considered "language handicapped." For this alone an army of special personnel is required. There are NE (non-English) co-ordinators, SAT's (supplementary assistant teachers), non-English speaking classes (2,099 in elementary schools, 259 in junior high schools, in 1958).

But the language difficulty may be the least of the factors affecting ability to learn—it does not seem to have been a great handicap for some other immigrant groups. Far more important apparently are aspects of home atmosphere, both as they bear directly on the general physical and psychological well-being of the child, and in setting up conditions of various kinds that aid learning. The absence of such conditions—parents who read, relatives who have professional jobs, home discussions of political events, exposure to cultural activities—probably counts for a great deal in the factors leading to poor educational results for Negro and Puerto Rican children. It is a tribute to American idealism, which seems to be convinced that every human problem is manageable, that even these defects in home environment are now the concern of the Board of Education, through its Demonstration Guidance Project and Higher Horizons Project. Under these projects, students who on the most generous interpretation seem to show prospects for doing good academic work are selected for special intensive efforts—testing, training, remedial work, guidance, and the like, including (in the case of Higher Horizons) trips to the opera and plays. Such investments of special effort have indeed been rewarding. They also mean a considerably heavier investment in the education of underprivileged children than in educating "other" children.

A good summary of the special effort being put into the schools with a high proportion of the underprivileged (primarily schools with high proportions of Negroes and Puerto Ricans) is provided by the figures on personnel now employed in "special service" schools (as they are called), as compared with the regular schools. The report compares some "special service" and other schools: the special service schools have 29 per cent more personnel than the regular schools. For every position, there is more staff in the "special service" schools. Thus, for example, in the junior high schools, 44 special service schools have 62.4 guidance positions, 82 other schools have 85.6 posi-

145

tions. The problem is now whether it is "more important" to have guidance for a child who may make a mistake in the choice of vocational high school than to have guidance for a child who may make a mistake in his choice of a college. It is difficult to say what a rational analysis, or a moral judgment, might conclude: but regardless of what they might conclude, the distribution of effort as between these two needs will be decided politically, and presumably the Board of Education is more concerned now with satisfying the parents of poor students that everything possible is being done to give their children the best education than it is in satisfying the parents of good students that everything possible is being done for *them*. The latter of course generally have alternatives.

As to the other objective indices of inferior education. Large numbers of new schools have been built in the mainly Negro and Puerto Rican sections of the city—indeed, walking through Harlem, one almost thinks that there are scarcely any old schools still to be replaced. The Board of Education now makes vigorous efforts to assign regular teachers to the "special service" schools. Regularly appointed teachers are now centrally assigned, and the special service schools now have a greater number of regular teachers than the other schools.[2] Indeed, since the substitute can still shop around for a job in the huge school system, while the regular teacher is assigned (as a result of one of the most important recommendations of the Commission on Integration), the current report points out that some substitutes are avoiding taking the regular teaching licenses so as to preserve their freedom!

[2] The special service schools have more regular teachers for a given number of students than the other schools do. However, since the special service schools have much larger staffs, their larger *numbers* of regular teachers form a smaller *percentage* of the total professional staff in these schools.

Yet all of this, one can predict, while it may mean better education and more service to the Negro and Puerto Rican children, will not get the Board of Education off the hook. *After* the report on all these efforts to promote integration came out, after it was pointed out that close to 30 per cent more professional personnel was being assigned to the special service schools, that these had a larger number of regular teachers, and that the new schools serving under-privileged areas would have and do have more of every-thing—lunchroom space and supplies, special facilities of all kinds, and the like,—after all this, the arrangements for a school strike continued to go ahead, as they had in 1958 and 1959, and James L. Hicks of the *Amsterdam News* (the most important Negro newspaper in the city) wrote:

> I opposed a school strike last year because I felt Dr. Theobald and Dr. Silver of the Board of Education could and would meet the demands of parents if given enough time. I know now that I was wrong. Dr. Silver and Dr. Theobald either could not—or would not—fully meet the demands made by Negro parents for better integrated schools for their children. I don't know if they could have or not.
>
> All I know is that Negro children are entitled to the same things white children are entitled to and they are not getting them and that it is the white people who are keeping them from getting what they are supposed to have.
>
> That's why if there is a strike this year I'm backing it all the way. . . .

This is not the reaction of all Negroes, for while the *Amsterdam News* was writing in this vein, the Pittsburgh *Courier* was in effect accepting the position of the Board of Education that relatively little could be accomplished through zoning, and the task was to make the education of

Negro children, in the de facto segregated schools, as good as possible. It commented in an editorial:

> New York City's School Superintendent John J. Theobald's report apologizing for the fact that so-called racially "segregated" schools have not disappeared from the system is no cause for either concern or grief.
>
> Indeed, this is inevitable considering that three out of five Manhattan students are either Negroes or Puerto Ricans, as are two out of five in the entire city.
>
> Things being what they are in the local labor market low-rent housing projects will continue to be occupied by low-income groups which largely consist of Negroes and Puerto Ricans; while high-rent housing will continue to be occupied by high-income groups, overwhelmingly white. . . .
>
> Despite all efforts of the school administration, there can be no increase in school integration as long as the present population trends continue—and we don't think it makes much difference, no matter what the professional integrationists say.
>
> The important consideration is that the schools be structurally adequate for the needs of the communities in which they are located; that the number and quality of teachers be adequate, and that the curricula not be inferior to that of schools in which most of the student bodies are white.
>
> Much of the professional integrationist "reasoning" is based on the fallacious assumption that learning aptitude is somehow improved by racial mixing per se.

But this is not likely to be the politically effective position. The difference between one professional staff person per 20 children and one per 30 children is hard to observe; the difference between an all-white school and an all-Negro school is easy to observe. The difference between a good education and a poor education is hard to test; the difference between one color and another is easy to see. The Pittsburgh *Courier's* position may comfort the Board of Education; but it still has to deal with Negro parents who will not send their children to all-Negro schools, regardless of what the Board of Education does for them, and regardless even of what the objective indices show. (The Board of Education report for 1958–59 points out that New York elementary school students—despite the fact that two-fifths of them are Puerto Rican and Negro, and one-tenth of them are language handicapped—score *ahead* of the national norm in mathematics. Graduates of New York academic high schools are still consistently better than the national average—but not many of the Negro and Puerto Rican students get to, or through, the academic high schools.)

We can understand this Negro reaction to all-Negro schools. Negro parents cannot take the position that Irish or Jewish or Italian parents took before them—all this will change. Their history is different, their situation is different, their sense of self-confidence and self-worth is different.

Even so, all parents are very much the same: the Negro parents who don't want their children to go to all-Negro schools are very much like the white parents who also don't want their children to go to all-Negro schools, and it is equally difficult to say that either prejudice or self-hatred is the whole story. In both cases, parents want the best educational environments for their children; they don't envisage the elementary school years as years in which their children must become precocious social workers, presenting models of good scholarship and good discipline in a sea of misery; parents would rather have their children go to schools in which they in turn were presented with good models to spur them to higher levels of achievement. It would be as wrong to say the motivation of the striking and distressed Negro parents is entirely to escape from their own kind as to say the motivation of the retreating white parents is entirely prejudice. In both cases there is a positive component; the desire to do the best one can for one's children.

But what is the Board of Education to do? It needs the few good children (more than a few) in each school—they are important for the morale of the principal and teachers, as well as of other students. One might ask, why is the Board of Education so insistent on maintaining the principle of the neighborhood school? Suppose it were to allow parents who wished to be responsible for getting their children to distant schools to make their own choice. Suppose it would, each year, set up a list of under-utilized schools: many of these schools are in "good" neighborhoods, with established teaching staffs; and suppose the Board were to say, parents may now send their children to one of these schools if they wish. The Board may be afraid that chaos would result—yet one could predict that the overwhelming majority of the parents in the schools with high concentrations of Negroes and Puerto Ricans would continue to send their children to the nearest school —most of them (like most other parents, but in even higher proportions) don't care enough about the education of their children to bother that much, and don't know enough about different schools to know what good it would do if they did bother. The same home conditions that produce poor students would act to prevent involvement of the kind that might lead, if there were some system of permissive zoning, to mass exodus and disruption of the school system.

But more important probably in the thinking of the Board of Education than such possible administrative disorder (though this must certainly play an important role in any such huge organization) is the fact that permissive zoning would strip the schools that need them most of their few good students to send them to schools that already have enough.

And there are two further difficulties to permissive zoning as a solution to the integration problem. The first is: how can the Negro and Puerto Rican parents be permitted to choose schools for their children and other parents not be allowed to do the same? And if this right is given to other parents, would not the effect be to "de-integrate" some schools that now have a large minority of "other" children?

Conceivably the Board could limit permissive zoning to schools that are overcrowded. This would permit parents of children in overcrowded schools with high concentrations of Negro and Puerto Rican pupils to send them to other schools, but it would do little to bring "other" children into the special service schools.

Indeed, there are good arguments for permissive zoning. For example, it seems silly for parents in a city with hundreds of schools to be required to send their children to just one, as if they lived in a village. If they have a choice of more jobs and more entertainments in a large city, why shouldn't they have a choice of more schools? And why shouldn't a conscious effort be undertaken to make the schools different and distinctive, instead of the same. But even though I prefer the greater freedom of such a system, I do not see, for the reasons I have discussed, how it would further integration.

I began by saying the matter is horribly complicated; I hope those who have followed me this far will agree.

Of course, if one takes a long-range view one can think of possible solutions. Eventually the impact of a fairly good school system, non-discriminatory renting, the movement of Negroes and Puerto Ricans into better jobs, will reduce the gap between Negro and Puerto Rican students and "other" students. In the meantime, the Board of Education, with the tacit consent of the people of the city, pours in heavy resources to make up for the disasters of history, trusting that in some way the injection of money and personnel at this end will overcome generations of misfortune. Even so, it is not likely to get much sympathy for its efforts from the victims of the misfortunes. But since when have victims been kind to anyone—to their persecutors, to those who tried to aid them, or to themselves?

[After this article was written, the New York City Board of Education began to allow parents from the segregated schools to transfer their children to certain undercrowded schools. This began in the higher grades in September 1960, and the program has been expanded each semester to include more grades and more schools. The response from Negro parents in taking advantage of this has been impressive, though not so extensive as to lead to the radical depopulation of the segregated schools. Studies are now underway testing the impact of the change on the education of the Negro children.]

Schools and Northern Negro Slums

JAMES B. CONANT

When one considers the total situation that has been developing in the Negro city slums since World War II, one has reason to worry about the future. The building up of a mass of unemployed and frustrated Negro youth in congested areas of a city is a social phenomenon that may be compared to the piling up of inflammable material in an empty building in a city block. Potentialities for trouble —indeed possibilities of disaster—are surely there.

Let me describe a slum that might be in any one of several of the large cities I have visited. The inhabitants are all Negroes and with few exceptions have entered the city from a state in the deep South any time within the last month to the last three years. Often the composition of a school grade in such an area will alter so rapidly that a teacher will find at the end of a school year that she is teaching but few pupils who started with her in the fall. I recall the principal of one school stating that a teacher absent more than one week will have difficulty recognizing her class when she returns. This comes about because mothers move with their offspring from one rented room to another from month to month and in so doing often go from one elementary school district to another. In one neighborhood a questionnaire sent out by the school authorities indicated that about a third of the pupils came from family units which had no father, stepfather, or male guardian. This particular section was by no means homogeneous, of course. For while many moved about from room to room, a quarter of the parents reported that they owned their homes. Only 10 per cent of the parents had graduated from high school and only 33 per cent had completed the elementary school. Contrast the situation in which a third of the parents have completed elementary school with that in a high-income suburb where as many as 90 per cent of the parents have bachelor's degrees, if not graduate degrees from a university.

These Negro slums seem to vary considerably with respect to the social mores. In some there are very bad gangs with gang warfare among the boys. There are also vicious fights outside of school between Negro girls. The condition in one such neighborhood was summed up by a principal of a junior high school who said even he was shocked by the answers to a questionnaire to the girls which asked what was their biggest problem. The majority replied to the effect that their biggest problem was getting from the street into their apartment without being molested in the hallway of the tenement. He went on to say that the area had a set of social customs of its own. The women, on the whole, work and earn fairly good wages, but the male Negro often earns less than the woman and would rather not work at all than to be in this situation. As a consequence, the streets are full of unemployed men who hang around and prey on the girls. The women are the centers of the family and as a rule are extremely loyal to the children. The men, on the other hand, are floaters, and many children have no idea who their father is. Similar reports from principals and teachers can be heard by the attentive and sympathetic visitor to the Negro slums of any one of several cities. Racial discrimination on the part of employers and labor unions is certainly one factor which leads to the existence of so many male Negro floaters.

What is terrifying is that the number of male youth in this category is increasing almost daily.

I have so far referred only to white and Negro slums. In some cities, New York in particular, there are slum areas inhabited by recent arrivals from Puerto Rico. In these sections, the problems are complicated by the difference in language. Unlike the American Negro from the South, these recent arrivals bring with them a set of social mores closely associated with their own methods of communication. At the same time, they often, if not always, come with children whose schooling has been bad. Clearly the task of educating these Puerto Rican children involves both a reading and a foreign language problem. Add to these problems the possibilities of interracial hostility and gang warfare between Negroes and Puerto Ricans and the resentment of both toward the whites, and one has a veritable witches' brew which comes to boil with unsavory violence in certain schools in certain areas—particularly in the junior high school years. The amazing feature of the whole situation is that pupils make any progress in schools in some areas of the city.

One needs only to visit such a school to be convinced that the nature of the community largely determines what goes on in the school. Therefore to attempt to divorce the school from the community is to engage in unrealistic thinking, which might lead to policies that could wreak havoc with the school and the lives of children. The community and the school are inseparable. For example, I have walked through school corridors in slum areas and, looking into classrooms, have seen children asleep with their heads on their hands. Is this situation the result of poor teachers without either disciplinary control or teaching ability? No, the children asleep at their desks have been up all night with no place to sleep or else have been subject to incredibly violent family fights and horrors through the night. Checking into one case, a principal said that after climbing six flights of a tenement he found the boy's home—one filthy room with a bed, a light bulb, and a sink. In the room lived the boy's mother and her four children. The social attitudes found in this kind of slum neighborhood are bound to affect the atmosphere of the school. As one Negro teacher said, "We do quite well with these children in the lower grades. Each of us is, for the few hours of the school day, an acceptable substitute for the mother. But when they reach about ten, eleven, or twelve years of age, we lose them. At that time the 'street' takes over. In terms of schoolwork, progress ceases; indeed many pupils begin to go backward in their studies!"

Those who are deeply concerned with the education of the children in these slum areas are not waiting for others to change the social setting in which the schools operate. They are tackling the problem of getting the boys and girls from the poorest families to learn to read and write and do arithmetic. Foreign languages in grade seven or algebra in grade eight have little place in a school in which half the pupils in that grade read at the fourth grade level or below. Homework has little relevance in a situation where home is a filthy, noisy tenement. Discipline, of course, is a problem. Many educators would doubtless be shocked by the practice of on-the-spot demotion of one full academic year, with no questions asked, for all participants in fights. In one junior high school, a very able principal found so intolerable a situation that he established that very rule. As a consequence, there are fewer fights in his school among the boys, many of whom at one time or another have been in trouble with the police. In this school and in many others like it one finds the boys wearing ties and jackets to school, if not their one Sunday suit. When spoken to in the classroom, they rise to recite. Passing time between classes may be as short as one minute in order to preserve order in the halls. The school attempts to bring some kind of order to otherwise chaotic lives. And what is important, this formal atmosphere, at least in one school I know of, appears to work. School spirit has developed, and efforts are now being made to enlist the interests of the parents in the education of their children, who must stay in school till they are sixteen and whom the school will try to keep in school till graduation to prevent unemployed, out-of-school youth from roaming the streets.

The Importance of the Home

In the slum school, the development of reading skill is obviously of first importance. The earlier the slow readers are spotted and remedial measures instituted, the better. Indeed, the same rule applies as well to any school, but in the heavily college-oriented suburb, the number of slow readers is relatively small and teaching children to read by no means looms so large and difficult a problem as it does in the slums. Some commentators have failed to recognize the relation of the reading problem to the socio-economic and cultural level of the home. Evidence on this point is found in the large cities. Essentially the same methods are used in all the elementary schools in a city, and yet the average grade level of reading in the sixth grade, for example, may vary as much as two grades from one school to another. Concern with improving the reading of the pupils, particularly the slow reader, must continue well beyond the elementary school.

Just how far up the reading scale one can hope to bring the majority of pupils in a slum neighborhood is an open question. The factors working against all forms of intellectual effort are powerful negative influences to overcome. Since the degree of influence of these negative factors varies from child to child even in the same neighborhood, and the neighborhood's social climate changes from year to year, sometimes from month to month, it would be very difficult to obtain significant figures if an analysis of the social factors were attempted. One can only report that in spite of the Herculean efforts which are being made, there are many ninth-grade students in certain large city schools —in some as many as a half—who are reading at a sixth-grade level or lower. It must be remembered, however, that because of the high family mobility very few of these youth have had the advantage of the special attention given to reading in the lower grades in the same city.

In one school the teachers themselves, mostly Negroes, felt that the only way to improve the reading of the children in the first three or four grades was to do something with their mothers. If the head of the family unit could be located and brought into communication with the school, attempts were made to stimulate an interest in newspapers, magazines, and possibly even books. One of the troubles, the teacher said, is that when the children leave the school they never see anyone read anything—not even newspapers.

In other all-Negro schools, this point was made again and again. Therefore many such schools use social workers or visiting teachers to keep the parent or parents in touch with the school. This is not always an easy task, for the almost illiterate parent may be frightened of anyone officially concerned with education. But if the parents can be induced to adopt a positive attitude toward the school, a first step has been taken. If the reading of some sort of printed material can be started, the way is open for the more usual forms of adult education courses. It may be that only by a greatly increased expenditure of funds on adult education can the present blocks to children's educational progress be removed in the most depressed areas of the large cities.

De Facto Segregation

A thorny subject of great concern to those interested in improving Negro education is the question of whether or not de facto segregation, as some like to call it, is detrimental to the education of the Negro. Closely related is a second question; namely, should the school authorities endeavor to move Negro children into purely white schools in order to have as many mixed schools as possible? The issue is a very real one, and in a sense it is primarily political. At this point, I must make reference to the Supreme Court decisions of 1954 and 1955 because of a tendency to regard them not only as the law of the land but as a sacred text on education. Clearly even a unanimous opinion of the Supreme Court fails to determine educational policy except within the framework set by the issues before the Court—in this case, the "segregation of children in public schools solely on the basis of race." It is necessary to point out this obvious fact, for I have heard the statement made that because the Supreme Court expressed the opinion that "separate educational facilities are inherently unequal," all completely Negro schools are morally wrong and that there is essentially no difference between de jure segregation still found in almost all Southern communities and what some call de facto segregation in portions of the large Northern cities.

If one turns to the Supreme Court decision in the case of Brown et al. v. Board of Education of Topeka [347 U.S. 483 (1954)], one finds the sentence I have just quoted about separate educational facilities. Taken out of context, the conclusion might be drawn that the justices declared separate educational facilities for whatever reason provided are morally wrong and if supported by tax funds are illegal. Yet on reading carefully the whole opinion, I think the key sentence is the question defined by the Court: "Does segregation of children in public schools *solely* on the basis of race, even though the physical facilities and other 'tangible' factors may be equal, deprive the children of the minority group of equal educational opportunities? We believe that it does." I have italicized the word "solely," as I presume to think it is the essential word. The justices appear to have expressed no view as to whether the pupils in a completely Negro school are deprived of equal education opportunity if they are not assigned solely because of their race. In short, if one group of children is separated from another group because of the neighborhood in which they live, the fact of this separation is, of and by itself, no evidence of an inequality in education. Whether in fact the facilities and instruction are equal in a 100 per cent white school, a mixed school, and a 100 per cent Negro school in a large city is to be determined by examining the schools, not by appeal to phrases such as de facto segregation with the implication that it is to be condemned by all right-thinking people who condemn de jure segregation.

In some cities, political leaders have attempted to put pressure on the school authorities to have Negro children attend essentially white schools. In my judgement the cities in which the authorities have yielded to this pressure are on the wrong track. Those which have not done so, like Chicago, are more likely to make progress in improving Negro education. It is my belief that satisfactory education can be provided in all-Negro schools through the expenditure of more money for needed staff and facilities. Moreover, I believe that any sense of inferiority among the pupils caused by the absence of white children can be largely if not wholly eliminated in two ways: first, in all cities there will be at least some schools that are in fact mixed because of the nature of the neighborhood they serve; second, throughout the city there ought to be an integrated staff of white and Negro teachers and administrators.

To insist that such solutions cannot be acceptable and to assume instead that the schooling of Negroes can be satisfactory only if in each schoolroom there are present some white children is to take an extremely defeatist view of Negro education in the large cities. The proposal to move any appreciable number of white children by bus into what are now Negro schools or to move all the Negro children in a Negro neighborhood into what are now white schools presents a transportation problem that is quite insoluble. An examination of the geography of the Negro and white sections of the large cities makes this evident. If some children are to be transported, the question arises which children and how many.

At the elementary school level the issue seems clear. To send young children day after day to distant schools by bus seems out of the question. It must be remembered that unless by the accident of population migration there are empty seats in the predominantly white schools, white children would have to be transported to Negro areas in order to free the necessary space. Clearly a complicated arrangement for moving large groups of young children around a city for the sake of mixing all the elementary schools is hardly worth discussing. At the high school level, the youth are certainly old enough to commute; one complication present in the elementary schools has disappeared. Still, a great network of transportation would have to be provided in a number of cities if the goal were to have every high school a mixed school. I have already noted the problem of determining the proper degree of admixture of white and Negro children. The more one considers the matter, the more one is convinced that children should not be manipulated for the purpose of seating Negro children in white schools or vice versa. To my mind, the city school superintendent is right who said he was in the education business and should not become involved in attempts to correct the consequences of voluntary segregated housing.

I know the argument is being made that crossing attendance lines should be permissive and without cost to the city and that the refusal of this right is a psychological blow to the pride of the members of the Negro race. But the reason for demanding such a privilege is the allegation that education in an all-Negro school to which pupils are not assigned solely on account of race is inherently inferior. Once this allegation is granted, the foundation for improving Negro education in the large cities is undermined. Since I believe the evidence indicates that it is the socio-economic situation, not the color of the children, which makes the Negro slum schools so difficult, the real issue is not racial integration but socio-economic integration.

Put another way, if there is no inherent difference in potential ability, and if educational opportunity is equal, the poor achievement of the children in both the Negro and white slums described earlier may be ascribed to their depressing cultural and socio-economic backgrounds. One might argue, therefore, that all slum schools ought to be integrated with schools in economically favored areas. If the body politic through its school board once sets out on a course of neighborhood desegregation, a good case can be made for transporting white children from slum schools to schools in high income residential districts and vice versa.

Much as I admire the comprehensive high school in the town with one high school and see it as an instrument of democracy, it seems impossible for school authorities in a large city to create artificially a series of such schools. If a policy were to be adopted that, as an ideal, every neighborhood school should have a widely heterogeneous school population represented by all socio-economic backgrounds, school administrators would be forced to move children about as though they were pawns on a chessboard.

Antithetical to our free society as I believe de jure segregation to be, I think it would be far better for those who are agitating for the deliberate mixing of children to accept de facto segregated schools as a consequence of a present housing situation and to work for the improvement of slum schools whether Negro or white. The problems in these schools are far more difficult to solve than in other schools, larger and better staffs should be available, more money is required. It is my firm belief that actions based on the premises I have outlined are in the best interests of the Negro and of the nation. Through the existence of at least some mixed schools, integrated teaching staffs, and increased expenditures in slum schools, I suggest that the education of Negroes in Northern cities can be made satisfactory and their status improved.

Mexicans in the United States
A Problem in Social Differentiation

LEONARD BROOM AND ESHREF SHEVKY

There are sharp limitations in detail of knowledge about the Mexican-American population in Southern California, its locality of highest concentration and differentiation. Among the special factors which seem to affect the integration of Mexicans into American society, and which require further research, are these:

Acculturation and Urbanization.

A number of factors have converged to retard the acculturation of Mexicans in the United States. The pattern of mass employment in which Mexicans worked in homogeneous gangs tended to insulate them from contacts with other ethnic groups. Although this was by no means peculiar to Mexicans, it is unlikely that gang employment was experienced by any other population in so many occupations and for so long.

Their position as casual laborers, linked with instability of employment and frequent migration, resulted in residential and institutional isolation. Both in rural and urban areas the ethnic enclaves were marginal neighborhoods detached from the life and economy of the large community, although dependent upon it for jobs and services.

Under these circumstances the language barrier which initially was an obstacle to relations between the group and American society became a persistent symbol and instrument of isolation. The language barrier effectively isolated a large part of the first generation and was an important factor in reducing the rate of naturalization. The second generation, very often confronted with learning English upon entering school, still suffers from retardation. Where no legal segregation existed the size of the Mexican population made possible administrative segregation. Retardation, in turn, imposed an educational ceiling on the group with the vicious circle consequences: limited schooling retarded acculturation, set arbitrary job ceilings, constricted job opportunities, and the group became symbolized by its stereotype.

In all populations where the immigrant group is predominant among adults, the strata of acculturation are age structured. The cleavage in the case of Mexicans in Southern California has gone so far that the second generation has become isolated from the parental group but has not secured access to the larger society. The formation of gangs of Mexican youth is an obvious manifestation of this condition. Through these gangs a critical period of the life span of the individual is ethnically delimited. Because of the cleavage from the parental generation and the age determination of youthful associations, the second generation enter adulthood with a dearth of appropriate models.

Status and Assimilation.

At first glance the constricted status of the Mexican-American group impresses the observer. Within the urban status system they occupy an apparently undifferentiated position, socially excluded, economically depressed, and politically powerless. Unlike other important American ethnic groups a middle class providing service functions is virtually nonexistent. Those individuals who have advanced substantially, either economically or in educational status, have tended to lose their identity with the group and have moved away from the ethnic enclaves which are entirely lower class. This movement is facilitated by the alternative definitions of "Spanish," "Colonial," "Californian," and the like, which do not carry the stigmatizing connotation of Mexican. The availability of alternative definitions provides a ready rationalization both for vertically mobile individuals and the host population and undoubtedly acts to reduce stress in transitional adjustment. In a higher status context the Spanish name carries even a prestige value and this is in contrast to the assimilating Jew, who often is confronted with the problem of name changing. Granting the economic and cultural prerequisites, color is the only arbitrary qualification to a ready change in Mexican self-definition. Vertical mobility and loss of identification as Mexicans should theoretically be easier for those who approximate the "Castilian type." It also remains to be discovered to what extent the factor of color is selective in affecting the permanence of settlement in the United States and the secondary movement of Mexicans in this country.

Some of the conditions present which might lead to development of further status differentiation of the Mexican-Americans as such are ethnic nationalism as expressed in the concept *raza*, Mexican patriotism, culturally modified Catholicism, and a persistent interest in the ancestral culture, this last finding reinforcement in the friendly attitudes toward Latin America shared with the general population. The convergence of these and other factors could conceivably result in the assimilated and vertically mobile elements remaining within the ethnic group.

Modes of Isolation and Integration.

Unlike the classic form of the Black Belt and European immigrant settlements, Mexican-American urban neighborhoods are not large, continuous concentrations. The initially diffused utilization of this segment of the labor force, in Southern California at any rate, gave rise to a number of relatively small homogeneous nuclei, marginal to but dependent upon urban centers and those subcenters performing industrial functions. Many of the disparate settlements were engulfed in the growth of the city, but were hardly modified by their change in relative position. Los Angeles, with the largest industrial concentration in this region, attracted the largest population of Mexican origin. Peripheral communities of seasonal agricultural workers are being changed by the processes of urbanization into marginal neighborhoods of urban workers. This change and the tendency toward a greater urban concentration and localization have manifold sociological consequences which are the preconditions for further differentiation of the population and for their mobilization for political action on a scale heretofore impossible.[1]

Under present conditions of isolation the service facilities of the group are rudimentary. For the most part, they are supplied by self-employed persons who operate marginal commercial enterprises functionally isolated from the mass economy. The chief service area catering to the Mexican-American population is located in the deteriorated urban center of Los Angeles. All important Mexican-owned enterprises are found here and, with all the risks involved, this is the entry point for independent commercial activity. The

[1] Mobilization for political action has begun to become a reality among Mexican-Americans, along with the development of organizational leadership. The Community Service Organization, patterned after the National Association for the Advancement of Colored People in its social action emphases, was formed in 1947 and by 1960 had 10 thousand members in 28 chapters in California and several in Arizona. Several figures of local political importance had emerged, and the CSO had achieved some of its political objectives in California, notably the extension of old-age pensions to long-residing non-citizens.

professional and semiprofessional personnel are also concentrated here, but the number and diversity of services rendered are even less adequate than is the case in Negro and Japanese-American neighborhoods.

Correlative with isolation and weakness are deficiencies of available capital and technical and professional skills. These conditions impede the integration and effective organization of the group. There is a dearth of personnel with sufficient resources or technical skills competent to cope with the bureaucracy of business enterprise or government. Strong leadership is unavailable either for periods of group crisis or for enduring community organization.

Despite the early significance of the mutual aid societies and the persistence of some of them over a period of years, they do not appear now to have any important place. Without exception, large immigrant populations in the United States developed this type of organization as an early and transitional form. In some cases the functions became incorporated in an institutional system within the ethnic group. Thus far, at least, this does not seem to have taken place among the Mexican-Americans despite the fact that the group has remained isolated and in large part culturally distinct.

Like the mutual aid societies the first trade unions with Mexican leadership were a transitional form. Although their original leadership participated in the series of agricultural strikes of the 1930's, no effective organization persisted. Incorporation of Mexicans in any numbers into the American labor movement awaited the development of stable industrial unionism in areas of Mexican employment. No other secular organization appears at this time to be capable of affecting so decisively the pattern of Mexican isolation. Depending on the composition of the "locals," unionization may have important bearing on the rate of acculturation, the character of interaction between Mexicans and other groups, and their participation in civic and political activities.

The church is the principal agency of cultural conservatism for Mexicans in the United States and reinforces the separateness of the group. This is true, whether one has in mind the parish organization of the Catholic Church or the Protestant missions with their functionally sectarian attributes. Competition between the church and the mission reveals and accentuates cleavages in the Mexican population and is an obstacle to consensus. When Mexicans become participants in Protestant denominational or nonethnic Catholic organizations the phenomenon is an aspect of vertical mobility and does not affect the isolation of the group.

The Adjustment of Puerto Ricans
to New York City

JOSEPH P. FITZPATRICK

In attempting to evaluate the role of prejudice in the adjustment of the Puerto Ricans in the next ten years, a number of factors affecting the life of Puerto Ricans on the mainland must be kept distinct, one from the other. First, it is important not to confuse prejudice against the Puerto Ricans with certain kinds of difficulties which are simply part of the problem of urban living for poor people whether they are Puerto Rican or not. There is danger both to Americans and to Puerto Ricans in identifying as prejudice something which is part of the routine of living in the modern city. Secondly, it is important not to allow certain temporary outbursts of prejudice which create temporary difficulties to blind us to the real issues in long-range adjustment. Thirdly, the major issues in long-range adjustment are partly cultural, partly racial. It is in terms of these two factors, cultural integration and racial integration, that the real issue of prejudice must be examined.

CONFLICTS OF INTERESTS

When a large group of newcomers move into a city, a great many differences arise which I call conflicts of interest.

The neighborhood is the main focus of this experience. For instance, the practice of converting apartments, readapting them into rooming houses or apartments and renting them to Puerto Ricans inevitably precipitates a conflict of interest. Prompted by a desperate need for housing, Puerto Ricans move in, to find themselves the object of bitter resentment on the part of older residents. Prejudice comes to play an important role, indeed, but the major role is a conflict of interests: the desire of a landlord to increase his profits; the need of Puerto Ricans for a place to live; and a concern of older residents for the preservation of their neighborhood.

A second experience of this nature is associated with relocation. I am fully aware that re-development can sometimes be a polite word for getting rid of Puerto Ricans, Negroes and others whom comfortable citizens do not want around. But in a city like New York, slum conditions pile up and deterioration leads to drastic action. Since many of the Puerto Ricans are in the poor housing, they are displaced, relocated, subjected to a great many inconveniences, which make life extremely difficult for them. In a very understandable cry against this inconvenience, it is not uncommon to speak of discrimination and prejudice. These elements are present, but many other elements are present also: the turmoil that has been associated with the city's life for generations; part of the death and re-birth that have marked the city's history, the demolition and rebuilding that has been pushing immigrants around the city for more than a hundred years.

A third experience of this nature is in the area of occupation. Newcomers become a threat to the jobs of older residents. In this situation Puerto Ricans are exploited. However, it would not be wise to confuse exploitation with prejudice. A person who exploits another is not concerned whether he is English, French, Puerto Rican or Scandinavian. If he can find someone of whom he can take advantage, he is remarkably unconcerned about racial or ethnic backgrounds. In fact, some of the most effective exploiters of immigrants were members of their own ethnic group. The poverty of Puerto Ricans, their language handicap, their lack of sophistication about mainland city life, leave them, at this moment, particularly exposed to exploitation.

In this regard, it is much more effective to minimize the factor of prejudice even though it may be there, and to guide the Puerto Ricans to a kind of positive action against the situation of exploitation in general. This will gradually be corrected by improved education, by social and economic advancement, by social and political organization and action.

These are some of the conflicts of interest, the trials that generally beset older residents and immigrants in a large and complicated city.

CONFLICTS OF CULTURE

There is a second area of conflict—a conflict of culture. When people of two different ways of life meet, serious difficulties arise for both. Gradually, in the United States, the migrating groups have lost the old way of life from which they had come, and have adopted a way of life that is characteristic of the United States. This is the process, so familiar to us, of immigrant assimilation.

The really serious aspect of the conflict of cultures is the distress it causes for the migrant or immigrant himself—his bewilderment in a world he does not understand, his confusion in the presence of customs and expectations that are strange to him. What was right in Puerto Rico, for instance, becomes wrong on the mainland; what was wrong in Puerto Rico becomes right on the mainland; the things that gave a man or woman dignity and honor in a Puerto Rican village are greeted with ridicule in New York. Parents never fully understand their children; children never fully

173

understand parents. Conflict between the generations may arise. Unless the family and the individual person are strong, life can become disorganized. Delinquency and mental breakdown may follow.

The conflict of culture affects the older residents in a different way. They find their own customs and way of life under pressure of strangers whom they do not understand. They fear the threat to their own values and traditions from people who are different.

The Color Question

Another possible impediment to speedy adjustment revolves around the troublesome issue of color. The adjustment of Puerto Ricans involves not only a question of cultural adjustment, but in many cases a question of racial adjustment for some Puerto Ricans who will be identified on the mainland as "colored."

The Puerto Ricans are the first group, migrating in large numbers to mainland cities, who bring with them a tradition of widespread social intermingling and intermarriage of people of noticeably different color. Two things may happen:

If this practice continues among the Puerto Ricans on the mainland, they may break the resistance to integration in mainland cities. If they can become established in mainland parishes and neighborhoods as a people that takes the intermingling of white and colored for granted, we should expect that the older residents will also gradually come to take for granted the intermingling of the two. Should the Puerto Ricans succeed in doing this, they would have brought to the mainland the extraordinary blessing of advancing the practice of acceptance of people regardless of their color.

However, another development may take place. Recognizing the handicaps of color on the mainland, the Puerto Ricans may gradually split into two groups: those who are taken as white becoming assimilated into the white community; those who will be considered colored becoming assimilated into the Negro community. If this happens, the Puerto Rican community will have become shattered; they will have lost their honorable tradition of non-discrimination; and the mainland cities will still be back where we would have been had Puerto Ricans never come.

The key factor in this problem is not the racial prejudice of mainland Americans. The existence of that and its manifestations are perfectly clear to everyone. The key factor in this will be the attitude of the Puerto Rican migrants themselves. It will involve their reflecting on the meaning of color in Puerto Rico; making explicit the values which have been implicit in customary behavior; and consciously facing the issue of color as they have never had to face it on the Island.

Two things are clear to anyone who is familiar with the culture of Puerto Rico: discrimination such as it exists on the mainland has not existed there; color is a matter of considerable anxiety for much of the population. It is not easy for a mainlander to reconcile these two things. The reason for it seems to be the following:

COLOR AND CLASS

In a two-class society of a traditional Spanish type, color became one obvious way of identifying a person as a member of the lower class. Once a person's identification with the lower class was clear, the factor of color did not mean much if it meant anything. It was only when a person developed aspirations for social advancement that color would become an issue. Obviously colored features were a drawback to social advancement. However, if a colored person was able, by his ability and his accomplishments, to distinguish himself, to become prominent, his higher class status would tend to overshadow his color. José Celso Barbosa, a colored man, founder of the Republican Party in Puerto Rico, claims in his writings that he never felt any disadvantage due to his color. His picture hangs in a prominent place in the Ponce City Hall. In other words, his position and his role in society subdued acknowledgment of his color. Steward, in his study of 200 top families in Puerto Rico indicates that a number of people in these top families had noticeable Negro or Indian features, but they were considered white.

Puerto Ricans generally explain the difference between the role of color on the mainland and in Puerto Rico as follows: On the mainland, the color of a person determines what class he will belong to; in Puerto Rico, the class a person belongs to determines his color. This is a puzzling principle for Americans to understand, but it can be illustrated abundantly in Puerto Rico's social life.

As Puerto Ricans come to New York, or indeed with the rapid rise of the middle class in Puerto Rico itself, Puerto Ricans face the serious question of re-defining the meaning of color. Color can no longer be simply a sign of lower class status. In New York, or in the middle class of Puerto Rican cities, what is color going to mean now? Will people continue to be accepted widely in social gatherings, in occupation, in housing, in marriage, regardless of their color? This would be to continue the marvelous tradition of non-discrimination. Or will they adopt the American pattern of discriminating on the basis of color, regardless of the value and greatness of the human person, and thus embrace the injustice and distress that discrimination has involved in our American culture?

What is more, in New York, Puerto Ricans will be caught immediately in the strong pressure for upward mobility, for social and economic advancement, and they will realize the handicaps that one must face in this regard if he is identified as colored on the mainland.

This has prompted a number of writers to conclude that the Puerto Ricans will split into two groups: those who will be identified as white; those who will become identified as colored. In order to determine whether this was happening, I did a study of the behavior of Puerto Ricans in six Catholic parishes in New York. I chose parishes of a wide variety of characteristics from the parish most heavily populated with Puerto Ricans to others where they are scattered widely and sparsely among older residents. Observation and interviews provided abundant evidence that the practice of Puerto Ricans of accepting the social intermingling of people of all colors was continuing up till that time in New York. A study of the marriages of Puerto Ricans in these parishes over a four-month period indicated that twenty-five percent of the Puerto Rican marriages involved people of noticeably different shades of color. This prompted the conclusion that the Puerto Ricans give strong evidence of continuing on the mainland the tradition of social relations between those of different color which is characteristic of the Island.

It seems clear, however, that if it is really going to continue, the Puerto Rican people themselves must make explicit the values on which their admirable social tradition is based. If they do, they will have brought a priceless contribution to the life of the mainland, and have succeeded in breaking, as no other group has done, the resistance to integration in mainland cities.

The Black Muslims in America

C. ERIC LINCOLN

The Black Muslims are not an isolated phenomenon. They are rooted in the whole structure of racial tension. In New York City alone, a score or more organizations operate in the name of black solidarity. Their central theme is always the glorification of black civilization and the deprecation of the white man's culture, which, whenever it has been adopted by the black man, has reduced him to impotence and ignominy.

In the South, where resentment of the white man has until recently been less overt, black nationalism has expressed itself in lodges and fraternal societies, in which tens of thousands of Negroes learn various "ancient rites" of supposed Afro-Asian origin. Every Negro community in the South has its multitude of legends illustrating the Negro's superior physical strength, sexual prowess and moral integrity. "Mr. Charlie" is never a match for the cunning of "Ol' John." And "Miss Ann," though she is "as good a ol' white woman" as can be found anywhere, remains in the mind of the Southern Negro a white woman and, therefore, a legitimate target for the petty machinations of her Negro servant, "Annie Mae."

Most Negroes do not, of course, spend most of their time "thinking black." But no part of Negro life is wholly free of this glorification. A defensive kind of black nationalism finds occasional expression in the quarrels of Negro children everywhere. "Black is honest," they cry out, and "the blacker the berry, the sweeter the juice." Even the Negro churches are often tinged with nationalism. An obscure African slave who rescued the prophet Jeremiah from a cistern into which he had been thrown by his enemies is exalted as a symbol of righteousness and fearlessness in the service of God. And the biblical promise that Ethiopia shall soon "stretch out her hands" is taken as a divine pledge that black sovereignty will be restored.

From the soil of repression and hostility grow bitter fruits, and black nationalism is one of the most bitter. It feeds on the prejudices, stereotypes, and discriminations which tend to characterize relations between whites and blacks in America. It accepts the white man's allegation that there are "inherent differences" between people who have different colored skins. But it inverts the values: it worships what it cannot change. It forges a weapon of vengeance for the Black Man out of the very attributes for which he is held to be inferior.

The Black Muslims have made a science of black nationalism. They have made black the ideal, the ultimate value; they have proclaimed the Black Man to be the primogenitor of all civilization, the Chosen of Allah, "the rightful ruler of the Planet Earth." And their extreme racist doctrine has attracted more than a hundred thousand adherents—a vivid warning of the deep resentment American Negroes harbor for their status in our society and of the futility they feel about the likelihood of a genuine and peaceful change.

Under the circumstances confronting him, the Negro is required to be "Negro" before—and sometimes to the exclusion of—anything else. At some point, therefore, he will inevitably be tempted to glorify that from which he cannot escape. He may repudiate the white man's stereotype, turn his eyes from the painful reality, and substitute for them an idealized self-image. Drawing on the political parallel, in which each state considers itself distinct from and superior to its neighbors, this attitude has come to be known as black nationalism.

In any technical sense, of course, it is inaccurate for American Negroes to adopt a black nationalist position. The term implies that they are—politically, culturally, ethnically, or racially—a distinct group. But this is emphatically not true. Politically they are Americans, as American as one can be (with the sole exception of the American Indian). Culturally they are merged into the American mainstream; as Lloyd Warner observes, they are "culturally more like the white 'old American' than (are) any other sub-groups in America."[1] Nor are they ethnically separated from other Americans, holding allegiance to an earlier shared culture. On the contrary:

The conspicuous feature of the Negro in America is that his aboriginal culture was smashed. . . . The importance of this basic fact for the Negro in America cannot be overestimated. It means in effect that the old types of social organization and all their derivations could not continue, but a new type of emergent adjustment derived from the new conditions would have to be established.

Nor, finally, are they racially distinct. "Race" is at best a nebulous term. There are no pure races, and it would be especially inappropriate to apply the term to the American Negro, who is at once African and Anglo-Saxon, Indian and French, Portuguese, Spanish, German and Italian—a composite of every major "racial stock" and every nationality of Western Europe.

W. E. B. DuBois observes that a common suffering, rather than a common biology or ethnic identity, has been

[1] W. Lloyd Warner and Leo Srole, *The Social Systems of American Ethnic Groups,* (New Haven: Yale University Press, 1945), p. 295

181

the important factor uniting the Negro in what is usually referred to as "nationalism."

The so-called American Negro group . . . while it is in no sense absolutely set off physically from its fellow Americans, has nevertheless a strong, hereditary cultural unity born of slavery, of common suffering, prolonged proscription, and curtailment of political and civil rights . . . Prolonged policies of segregation and discrimination have involuntarily welded the mass almost into a nation within a nation. . . .

The "nationalism" of the American Negro is not voluntary, prompted by a desire to set himself apart in order to preserve some cultural values. It is, rather, a defensive response to external forces—hostile forces which threaten his creative existence. It is a unity born of the wish not to conserve but to escape a set of conditions.

Black nationalism seizes the conditions of disprivilege and turns them to advantage as a tool for eliminating the disprivilege. It challenges the supercilious attitude of the majority group by glorifying the unique symbols of the blacks—symbols which the whites consider repugnant. Some sociologists have labeled this behavior "negritude":

. . . an exaltation of African-Negro specificity, a "kind of highly elaborated counterracism." . . . It involves a "particularly intense racial awareness," not uncoupled to political activity and demands. It is a term descriptive, also, of an appreciation of a new black unity experienced by its adherents, a consciousness of sharing in a past and in the making of the future. . . .

Black Nationalism and Social Class:

In the American Negro groups of highest and lowest status, hardly anyone wants to be a Negro. Upper-class Negroes seek to identify themselves with the white society;

lower-class Negroes prefer to identify themselves with any group except the whites in order to escape the danger and humiliation that all Negroes incur. Only middle-class Negroes are generally willing to acknowledge themselves as Negroes and, at the same time, to seek an accommodation with the white society. Black nationalism, therefore, with its repudiation of both Negro identity and white culture, sinks its roots deepest in the lower class.

The Negro of the upper class is largely committed to the idea that America's racial dilemma will be resolved when the Negro loses his distinctiveness, social and biological. He would prefer to become so thoroughly assimilated into the American mainstream as to be biologically indistinct, for his new status could not then be revoked or qualified in a future crisis. In short, the ultimate security in living among a white majority is to be white. But this security is almost impossible to achieve in view of the general disdain for miscegenation. The barrier is circular; unqualified social acceptance is the only gateway to racial anonymity, which in turn is the only gateway to unqualified social acceptance.

For the time being, therefore, the upper-class Negro is settling for that degree of assimilation which will make him socially indistinct from those whites who are his counterpart in terms of education, affluence and refinement. He tends to venerate everything that is "white" and "Western." In spite of the inconvenience of his color, he sees himself as part of this tradition; and he resents as irrational and unjust the social custom which emphasizes his black skin while overlooking the fact that his ancestry is partly European and his culture totally Western.

The members of the growing Negro middle class are least concerned about disestablishing themselves as Negroes. They ridicule the upper class as "neurotic submarginals" who make themselves ridiculous in trying to attract the white man's attention. Nor can they see the importance of having white ancestry, since almost all American Negroes share this qualification to some degree. Besides, white ancestry is not a criterion of the white man's judgement when he erects barriers to set himself apart from all others. Segregation is directed at a class, not at members within it; and all Negroes, whatever their names, ancestry, or skin color, belong by definition to the segregated class.

The Negro middle class is somewhat ambivalent about black nationalism. The black nationalist's emphasis on a united struggle against subordination has a certain appeal, but the rejection of Negro identity and the search for cultural roots in Afro-Asian traditions have little or no appeal. The middle-class Negro feels no need to be either "Asiatic" or "European." He accepts the designation "American Negro" with no particular sense of opprobrium, and often with a certain pride, for he thus identifies himself with America's most important minority—a minority which has distinguished itself, in a brief span of history, by an achievement of progress unequaled by either "Europeans" or "Asiatics."

The self-image of the Negro middle class is one of ability and militancy, uncontaminated by either sycophancy or hatred for the white man. The middle-class Negro is not obsessed with status pretensions, as is the upper class, nor does he suffer the abject despair of the Negro masses. As a result, he seldom displays the kind of insecurity that needs to search for ancestral pegs upon which to hang a claim for present status and acceptance.

The main appeal of all black nationalist movements, then, is to the Negro lower class. Here the Negro's resentment is crystallized and open. He has long despaired of the white man's justice and of the trustworthiness of the "acceptable" Negro leaders who court the white man's favor. Moreover, he is already at the bottom of the ladder, so his economic and social position is not vulnerable. An indiscreet word, an admission of hostility or an identification with "radical" or "extremist" groups can cost him nothing. What has he to lose if the demagogues of black nationalism fan his resentment into hatred, openly expressed in defiance of all white men and their compliant Negro "friends"?

The lower-class Negro lives in a no man's land between two alien worlds, both of which he spurns. Unlike his upper-class brother, he has no conscious desire to be white or even "like the whites," whom he identifies with most of his misfortunes. But neither will he accept the implications of being "Negro"—a white man's word, which he sees as an epithet of contempt. The black race has a rich cultural heritage, extending thousands of years into the past; but the black men who were torn from their homes and shipped to the New World in chains were carefully isolated from that heritage. The history of the "Negro" begins in the torments and degradation of slavery in America. Unlike his better-educated brothers, the lower-class Negro is not generally aware that his ancestors served their new nation with distinction and that the term can be accepted with confidence—indeed, with pride. He is agonizingly aware of what "Negro" implies to most Americans, its humiliating connotation of white supremacy.

The lower-class Negro is ripe for the lure of black nationalism. He is proud to rediscover himself as a Black Man, linked to the great and venerable civilizations of the "single black continent" of Afro-Asia. He is grateful for a mystique, especially one dignified as religion, that rationalizes his resentment and hatred as spiritual virtues in a cosmic war of good against evil. And he is jubilant at his new vision of the future—a future not of racial equality, for which he believes the white man has shown himself unfit, but of black supremacy. For "black" to the black nationalist, is a quality and symbol of all that is glorious, triumphant and divine.

FUNCTION AND DYSFUNCTION

The Black Muslims, though they scrupulously obey all the laws which govern American citizens, do not consider themselves Americans at heart. They are a separate people, citizens of the Black Nation, joyously obedient to the laws of Allah as interpreted by his Messenger, Elijah Muhammad. To affirm and support the functional structure of American society—the fabric of mutual interrelationships that holds our many groups and subgroups together—is the furthest thing from their mind. Yet it is essential for us to evaluate the Movement, at least tentatively, in terms of its impact upon the organic unity of our society. Only in this way can we begin to understand what challenge we are facing and how we must respond.

Such an evaluation can never be definitive or precise. For example, America is not perfect, and attempts to cure its imperfections may take the form of serious intergroup conflict. Is this social conflict functional? Robert K. Merton holds that it is, so long as it aims at adaption and adjustment within the system, not apart from it. This seems to be reasonable, but other observers disagree; and in any case, the line between functional and dysfunctional social conflict remains hazy. Nor is this the only difficulty. The same social phenomenon may often be seen as both functional and dysfunctional (that is, as tending to shatter the organic unity of the society). To identify it as functional or dysfunctional, one must try to estimate its ultimate impact on the social fabric. Such a judgement is hazardous at best. Moreover, every broad evaluation of a group in these terms is inescapably subjective, since the benchmark is the observer's own perception of the nature and limits of our society as an organic whole.

For all these reasons and more, the functional and dysfunctional aspects of the Black Muslim Movement are not always easy to assess. But an attempt must be made. The Muslims are growing daily in size and power, and they are determined to have an impact on our entire way of life.

The Black Muslim Movement is functional for its membership, for the entire Negro community, and for the society as a whole in its insistence upon high standards of personal and group morality. It encourages thrift, cleanliness, honesty, sexual morality, diet control, and abstinence from intoxicating liquors, and it effectively re-established a center of authority in the home. Muslims are expected to hold steady jobs, to give a full day's work for their pay, and to respect all constituted authority. As a result, the Movement reduces adult and juvenile delinquency and strengthens its members' sense of independence and self-respect.

At a deeper level, the Movement provides outlets, short of physical violence, for the aggressive feelings aroused in its members by the callous and hostile white society. Muslims tend to be Negroes for whom the pressures of racial prejudice and discrimination were intolerable, whose increasing resentment and hatred of the white man demanded release. Unable to rationalize their deprivations (as Negro intellectuals do) and unable to find relief in the Christian church or any secular institution, they might well have followed the downward paths open to the despairing everywhere—the paths of crime, drunkenness, dope addiction, prostitution, and wanton violence, directed indiscriminately against the oppressors or displaced senselessly against others of the oppressed. As Muslims, however, they find a "safe" outlet for their tensions in verbal attacks on the white man and in powerful demonstrations of group solidarity. Indeed, the Movement is most clearly functional in its regeneration of men and women who, having despaired of more creative possibilities, found themselves enslaved to destructive habits and lost to social usefulness.

The religious awakening which the Movement brings to its adherents is also functional for the entire society. Many Muslims had previously been affiliated with no religion; others had been Christians, but found their needs unmet by the characteristic expressions of the contemporary church. On the whole, it is better for society for its dissatisfied elements to be associated with some religion rather than with none. (The specific religious doctrines of the Movement are, of course, irrelevant here. The organic unity of American society is not threatened by such articles of faith as the Muslims' respect for the Quran as the word of Allah or their belief in Fard as divine.)

In several important ways, the Muslims tend to strengthen the dignity and self-reliance of the Negro community. They are proving dramatically that a new, positive leadership cadre can emerge among American Negroes, at the grass-roots level. The Muslim schools are emphasizing Negro history, Negro achievements, and the contributions of Negroes to the world's great cultures and to the development of the American nation. These facts are rarely taught in public schools, and the Muslims may be alone in trying to bring the Negro community to an awareness of its racial heritage. Again, the Muslims' "buy black" policy is creating some new opportunities for Negro business and professional men—opportunities which are almost universally denied them in the wider community.

The Black Muslims do not, of course, want the Negro community to share its new-found skills and creative energies with the despised white man. But their drive to make the Negro aware of his own potential is nevertheless functional. Despite the Muslims' appeal for separation, a Negro community awakened at last to dignity and self-reliance will be ready to insist upon its status as an equal partner in the American democratic enterprise.

Finally, the very existence of the Muslims—their extreme black nationalism and their astonishing growth and vitality—is functional to the extent that it forces the larger, Christian community to face the reality of racial tensions, to acknowledge its own malfeasance, and to begin a spiritual and moral reform. The Muslims' dramatic expression of racial solidarity may shock the white man into realization that Negroes will no longer permit their just demands to be casually shrugged aside. Indeed, Muslim extremism may even rebound and actively assist the forces of integration. It may, for example, force a white reappraisal of other protest organizations, such as the NAACP, which are now widely resisted as "too pushy" or "radical." If these groups come to be seen as relatively conservative, if they gain increasing white support, and if the great surge of Negro protest is constructively channeled as a result, the Muslims will have proved integrative despite themselves. But this possibility hangs upon a slender thread—the hope that America will take the warning and act to save itself in time.

The Black Muslims' virulent attacks on the white man may prove to be a useful warning, but they are deeply dysfunctional in the most immediate sense. They threaten the security of the white majority and may lead those in power to tighten the barriers which already divide America. The attacks create guilt and defensiveness among both Negroes and whites, and offer to extremist elements on both sides a cover for antisocial behavior. Above all, the attacks promote a general increase in tension and mutual mistrust. Calm heads might see the Muslims as a timely warning; jittery and frightened men are more likely to lash back in an unreasoning and potentially explosive panic.

These attacks on the white man may also have tragic consequences for international relations. Americans tend to take for granted that the rising nations of Afro-Asia are Moslem, but few of us have a clear knowledge of even the major tenets of the Moslem faith. If the Black Muslims become accepted here as a legitimate Moslem sect, their doctrines—including their hatred of the white man—may well be mistaken for orthodox Moslem doctrines, at least by the rank and file. In that case, the true Moslem ideal of panracial brotherhood would either remain generally unknown or else be considered an all-too-familiar hypocrisy.

About the Authors

SEYMOUR MARTIN LIPSET is Professor of Sociology at the University of California at Berkeley. He received his Ph.D. from Columbia University, taught there and at the University of Toronto. He has been Ford Research Professor of Political Science and Sociology at Yale University and visiting professor at the University of Berlin, the University of Warsaw, and the Salzburg Seminar in American Studies. He is the author of *Political Man*, *Agrarian Socialism*, and (with M. Trow and J. S. Coleman) *Union Democracy*, (with Reinhard Bendix), *Social Mobility in Industrial Society*, and editor of *Society in America* by Harriet Martineau, (with Reinhard Bendix) of *Class Status and Power* and (with Leo Lowenthal) of *Culture and Social Character*.

JOSEPH S. HIMES is Professor of Sociology in the North Carolina College at Durham. He received his Ph.D. from Ohio State University. He has been Research Director for the Urban League of Columbus, Ohio; an editorial and feature writer for the Ohio State News and a postdoctoral Faculty Fellow of the Fund for the Advancement of Education at the University of California at Berkeley. In 1961–62 he was Fulbright Lecturer in Sociology at Helsinki University. He is author of *Social Planning in America* and numerous articles and reviews in professional journals.

CHARLES U. SMITH is Professor of Sociology and chairman of the sociology department at Florida A & M University. He is a graduate of Tuskegee Institute, received his M.A. from Fisk University and was the first Negro to receive a Ph.D. from Washington State University. He is president of the Tallahassee Council of Human Relations. He has published numerous articles on race relations.

MORTON GRODZINS is Professor of Political Science at the University of Chicago. He received his Ph.D. from the University of California at Berkeley. He has served as editor of the University of Chicago Press, Dean of the Division of Social Science, and Chairman of the Department of Social Science at the University of Chicago. He has served as consultant to a number of governmental bodies, including the President's Commission on National Goals in 1960. His publications include *Americans Betrayed; The Loyal and the Disloyal; Government and Housing in Metropolitan Areas*, and numerous articles.

DAN W. DODSON is director of the Center for Human Relations and Community Studies at New York University. He received his Ph.D. from New York University. He has been Editor-in-Chief of the Journal of Educational Sociology since 1943. Between 1944 and 1947 he served as director of the Mayor's Committee on Unity in New York City. During that time he advised with the Brooklyn Baseball Club in breaking the color line in baseball. He served as a consultant in the desegregation of the Washington, D.C. schools. Recent studies of his include "Racial Imbalance in the New Rochelle, New York Public Schools," "The Y.W.C.A. in a Changing Era," and "Power Versus Process in Community Organization, A Study of Chelsea Neighborhood in New York City."

About the Authors

NATHAN GLAZER has taught sociology at the University of California at Berkeley, Bennington College, and Smith College. He received his Ph.D. from Columbia University. He is the author of *American Judaism; The Social Basis of American Communism* and (with David Reisman and Reuel Denney) *The Lonely Crowd*. He has been an editor of *Commentary* magazine, and has written extensively on the problems of minority and ethnic groups in America as well as on other subjects.

JAMES B. CONANT is an internationally known scientist, educator, and statesman. President of Harvard University for twenty years, he served as U. S. High Commissioner to Germany and as a U. S. Ambassador in the postwar years. He has recently been engaged in studies of the American high school and of the education of American teachers under a grant from the Carnegie Foundation. He has written more than a dozen books, including *Modern Science and Modern Man; The American High School Today*, and *Education in a Divided World*.

LEONARD BROOM is Professor of Sociology and chairman of the Department of Sociology at the University of Texas. He received his Ph.D. from Duke University. He taught at Kent State University and at the University of California at Los Angeles, where he served for a number of years as chairman of the Department of Sociology. He is the author (with Philip Selznick) of *Sociology*, and of numerous articles.

ESHREF SHEVKY is Professor of Sociology and Anthropology Emeritus at the University of California at Los Angeles. He received his Ph.D. from Stanford University. He has conducted a number of regional studies for the government; for five years was chief of a survey division of the U. S. Department of Agriculture; and for another five years was consulting sociologist for the Haynes Foundation in Los Angeles. He is the author of a number of social area studies.

REV. JOSEPH P. FITZPATRICK, S.J., is Associate Professor of Sociology and Industrial Relations and chairman of the Department of Sociology and Anthropology at Fordham University. He received his Ph.D. from Harvard University. He has been a regular summer lecturer at the Catholic University of Puerto Rico, and has served as President of the American Catholic Sociological Society. He has been engaged in a special study of the problems of the Puerto Rican population in New York City and has published a number of articles on that subject, and on a wide range of other social problems.

C. ERIC LINCOLN is Professor of Social Philosophy at Clark University. He received his Ph.D. from Boston University. Trained in social science and the law, he is an ordained Methodist minister. *The Black Muslims in America* was the result of at least three years of intensive study and research. He has published a number of articles on race relations.

EARL RAAB has written on, taught, and been actively engaged in the field of intergroup relations. He has served on the governing bodies of the National Community Relations Council and the National Association for Mental Health, is now an officer of the California Fair Practices Committee, Chairman of the San Francisco-Bay Area Human Relations Clearing House, and Associate Director of the San Francisco Jewish Community Relations Council. A graduate of City College in New York with

About the Authors

post-graduate work at the University of California at
Berkeley, he has taught at San Francisco State College
and has lectured extensively. His publications include
Major Social Problems (with Gertrude Jaeger Selznick),
The Anatomy of Nazism, and numerous periodical
articles.

ANCHOR BOOKS

AMERICAN HISTORY AND STUDIES

ANCHOR BOOKS

Sociology (*continued*)

Sociology (continued)

40-200